When Gwendolyn Kills

Jessi Dillard

Published by Trellis Publishing, 2021.

WHEN GWENDOLYN KILLS

First edition. July 16, 2021.

ISBN: 979-8224554287

Written by Jessi Dillard.

WHEN GWENDOLYN KILLS

Jessi Dillard

In 1986, a troubled young woman named Gwendolyn Graham left her home state of Texas for Grand Rapids, Michigan. There, she took a position caring for elderly patients as a nurses' aide at Alpine Manor Nursing Home, under the supervision of a woman named Cathy Wood.

It didn't take long for the relationship between the two women to grow from a professional working relationship to a budding friendship – and even less time for that friendship to become romantically charged. Within just two years, the duo took their partnership even further, and were charged in 1989 with the smothering deaths of five of their female senior patients: 60 year old Marguerite Chambers, 95 year old Myrtle Luce, 79 year old Mae Mason, 74 year old Belle Burkhard, and 97 year old Edith Cook.

The couple earned themselves the nickname The Lethal Lovers, but according to Cathy Wood, their murderous spree was primarily planned and executed by Gwendolyn herself.

Blurring the lines

Cathy was recently divorced, having ended a marriage of seven years to her high school sweetheart, shortly after taking a position at Alpine Manor. Although she moved up the ranks at the nursing home quite quickly, her social life remained relatively stagnant – she had put on weight during her unsatisfactory marriage, and by the time she'd hit 450 pounds, her self-esteem was at an all time low.

Then, Gwendolyn Graham came along. The two women instantly hit it off, and together, they started exploring a new lesbian lifestyle. They were checking out Michigan's gay bar scene, partying all the time, and even experimenting with rough sexual play.

"There was a core group of nurses' aides there, they would socialize together, and many of them were gay – they spent a lot of their time hanging out at gay clubs," said Lowell Cauffiel, a crime author who wrote about the couple in a book titled 'Forever and Five Days.' "And Cathy became quickly caught up in that whole social world."

Cathy had gotten pregnant at the age of 17, and after giving birth, found herself unable to bond with her new baby. She started to withdraw from her family, refusing to spend time with her baby or her husband, and refusing to do anything to help out around the house.

"She didn't really want to be a mom – she wanted to be the center of attention. And it's hard to be the center of attention when you're home alone with just a child and a husband," Cauffiel said.

Her ex-husband, Ken, had encouraged her to take the job at Alpine Manor to try and shake her out of her apparent depression. Instead, he'd opened the door for his wife to pursue a relationship altogether.

"(Cathy) had found, in a lesbian relationship, the ability to communicate in a way that she never had with her husband," said Dr. John Palmatier, developmental psychologist, in a true crime documentary account of the case that aired on the Investigation Discovery channel.

"She was on an equal par with her partner, and found it much more rewarding than a heterosexual relationship."

As Cathy continued to pull away from her marriage, Ken began noticing the dark side his wife had kept hidden for many years.

"After time, he begins to see some of the little mind games she plays with him," Cauffiel said, "...the kind of mind game that Cathy pulls with everyone, no matter who she comes in contact with, in order to create chaos around people where she can reign queen in the middle of all the drama."

Ken moved out, taking their daughter with him, after Cathy demanded a divorce in August, 1986. Cathy wasn't bothered at all – she'd have more time and space to focus on her blossoming relationship with Gwen.

"Gwen worked in the nursing home, I didn't pay her much attention. But one day, I was sitting in the break room and Gwen walked in and that's the first time I noticed her scars," Cathy said. "So, I started watching her a little bit – she made me feel pretty, she made me feel special. She would do things that I wanted to do."

Police Chief Walt Sprenger told the Williamson Daily News in 1998 that the women's intimate involvement was a key factor in their eventual killing spree, "part of a complex web that brings the whole thing together."

"Just talking about murder got them both excited," stated a report about the murders that aired on TruTV. "The linked pain and pleasure of their sexual games became threaded with the idea of cruelty."

The two women continued their relationship for the next nine months, until Gwen suddenly picked up and moved back to her hometown of Tyler, Texas. And Cathy calls her ex-husband with some strange news.

"I wasn't supposed to say anything about it."

On October 6, 1988, Ken Wood strode into the Walker, Michigan Police Department and told the authorities what Cathy had told him.

"Ken Wood proceeded to tell me that his ex-wife had been involved in some homicides at a local nursing home," said Tom Freeman, a retired member of the Walker Police Department.

According to Ken, Cathy had confessed to him that she and another nurses' aide at the Alpine Manor had killed five women during the winter of 1987. The officers sat quietly and allowed Ken to tell his story, but were hesitant to put much faith in it – after all, it was entirely possible that the spurned ex-husband could be fabricating these bold allegations to get revenge on the woman who broke his heart.

However, Tom Freeman felt there could be something there. After running background checks on both Ken and Cathy Wood – which turned up no criminal history – the department reached out to the police in Tyler, Texas. Gwen Graham, as it turned out, had an outstanding misdemeanor warrant for her arrest, a result of writing some bad checks about three years earlier. Still, no record of previous violent activity.

The next step was to obtain a search warrant for the nursing home where Ken claimed his wife had murdered her patients. At Alpine Manor, police began examining employee and patient records.

"We were most interested in some of the patients that passed away while Gwen Graham and Cathy Wood were working together," said Roger Kaliniak, another since-retired member of the Walker Police.

The first questionable death police found was on January 18, 1987, when a patient named Marguerite Chambers – who'd lived at the facility for the past five years – died suddenly. Marguerite was just 60 years old, but the cause of death was listed as "natural." Just one month later, a 95 year old woman named Myrtle Luce suffered a fatal "heart attack."

"Gwen told me that she was going to do her – that's how we said it – do her so that no one would ever overhear, and if they did overhear, I was supposed to say it was a joke," Cathy said. "I wasn't supposed to say anything about it."

The next death came after less than a week – a nurses' aide unexpectedly found 79 year old Mae Mason dead on February 16.

"Cause of death for Mae Mason was a cardiac arrest. She was also suffering from Alzheimer's," said Roger. "The nurse on duty checked two hours before and found that she was okay. Two hours later, she was dead."

Over the next few weeks, hospital records indicated that two other female patients – Belle Burkhard and Edith Cook – passed away alone in their rooms.

"Most people who go into nursing homes leave nursing homes that way, and 99% of the time, there's never an autopsy or medical examination," Cauffiel said.

"There was no increase, whatsoever, in the number of deaths that they had when Gwen Graham and Cathy Wood worked there," said James Piazza, defense attorney. "So, there's nothing to show that these people were murdered."

But when detectives compared the dates of the deaths to the hours Gwen and Cathy were supposedly working, they discovered that everything matched up. According to Roger Kaliniak, it all "started to come together."

Next, investigators began interviewing Cathy and Gwen's co-workers – hoping to find out if any of them had ever witnessed anything suspicious or unusual.

"When Cathy and Gwendolyn first started at Alpine Manor, everybody thought they were okay people, but however, you know, after a period of time, they got to be – in my opinion – a little leery of both of them," Roger said. "They played a lot of games."

According to Cauffiel, many of these games were instigated by Cathy – who'd had plenty of experience with manipulation and mind games. One of their favorite games was to switch patients around between rooms in an attempt to confuse the rest of the nursing home staff.

"Cathy seemed to get a thrill out of stirring up trouble," Cauffiel said. "Planting little half-truths among people, keeping the place in turmoil, keeping the place in drama. She seemed to get a kick out of exerting control over people's lives."

While many co-workers said Gwen and Cathy's antics often went beyond harmless pranks, their responses were mixed when police asked if they thought the duo had been capable of killing five of their patients.

"Some of the co-workers thought that possibly, these murders did occur, and some didn't believe it," Roger said. "They didn't think that they were capable of doing that."

Tom decided it was time to talk directly to Cathy. According to Tom, she was working that day, so detectives brought her down to the station for an interview. At first, she tells investigators that the entire thing was a joke – a made up story that she'd told her ex-husband simply to get a rise out of him.

"I said, 'I don't believe it was a joke,' and after interviewing for more than 40 minutes, she finally (said), 'well, he didn't make it up, but I wasn't involved, it was Gwen Graham," Tom said.

Cathy eventually tells police the same story she'd told her ex-husband. According to her version of the events, the murders were Gwen's idea. She would roll up a washcloth and place it over the nose and mouth of her victim, pressing down just hard enough to smother them to death.

She killed them in order to "relieve her tension," Cathy explained. According to her, Gwen would suffer extreme stress, but after killing someone, she would always feel better.

The murders are what forensic psychologist Dr. Michael Abramsky describes as "thrill killings" – an expression of a "deviant personality," committed purely for "excitement."

"Gwendolyn Graham suffers from two co-existing personality disorders. She suffers from borderline personality disorder, and she has a great many psychopathic features," he said. "What that means is that she is chronically unstable in terms of her mood, and her interpersonal relationships will vacillate without reason – from good to bad, from love to hate, from happy to sad. She will commit acts against people, aggressive acts, antisocial acts, against other individuals."

Scarred for life

"After the fifth grade, my parents moved to Texas and we lived there, really, most of my teenage years," said Gwen, recalling her childhood growing up on a farm just outside of Tyler.

She was raised with what Lowell Cauffiel refers to as a "country psychology." Her father believed it was important for children to be exposed to life and death – to learn where their food came from, and how animals became that food. According to Cauffiel, Gwen frequently watched as pigs were slaughtered or chickens were beheaded.

He feels it had a lasting impact on Gwen.

"Her father had ordered her brother to kill Misty, her little dog who she loved very much, because she had barked at a horse, which had resulted in the rider being thrown," he said. "Gwen went out, dug up the dog, and saved its teeth and its skull in a little alabaster heart box, which she carried with her."

Her father also believed that children would grow up to be weak if they were held too often by their mothers as babies – and as a result, Gwen's mother showed her little affection. According to Cauffiel, Gwen was untouched by her mother for most of her very early development.

And according to Gwen, her father eventually became a violent substance abuser who sexually molested her – trauma that may support a psychiatric diagnosis of borderline personality disorder. Gwen also bears physical marks of the disorder, in the form of scars. Cauffiel said many people with borderline personality disorder seek grounding in the form of burning or cutting, since they often feel as though they are "falling apart."

Gwen Graham, he said, has 31 different scars up and down both arms.

"These are cigarette burns, and I have cuts, a few," Gwen said. "They were done when I was 16, I was angry for being molested and I did it in an effort to make myself ugly so it wouldn't happen again."

By the time she reached age 22, Gwen was ready to leave home. She moved to Grand Rapids, Michigan, and found a position as a nurses' aide at the Alpine Manor Nursing Home. There, she met Cathy Wood – who'd grown up in dysfunction of her own. However, according to Cauffiel, the only account of Cathy's childhood is from how she describes it.

"The way she portrays it is that she was unloved – her mother was very harsh on her, their father was physically abusive, and that she had very few friends," Cauffiel said.

Developmental psychologist Dr. John Palmatier said Cathy was diagnosed with both pathological personality disorder and narcissistic behaviour – a type of self-centeredness where others aren't seen as individual people, but rather as extensions of the narcissist's own needs.

"You see people as they're only good to you for what you can get from them, and that you are better than everybody else," said Abramsky. "It's kind of a grandiosity, where the rules don't apply to you."

Almost immediately, Cathy and Gwen bonded in a strange, intense way. According to Abramsky, the pair shared similar personality types – but while Gwen was a directly aggressive person with a tendency to act out, Cathy was more sophisticated and manipulative.

"Cathy's a sick mind – she'd say anything."

Gwen's aggression first began to manifest in late January of 1987, Cathy told detectives. At that time, she said, Gwen was getting more physical and more violent – and that after Gwen killed Marguerite, she forced Cathy to help while she killed additional patients. According to Cauffiel, Cathy served as the lookout, positioned at the door to the room where Gwen was committing the murder.

Supposedly, he added, Gwen would leave washcloths in her back pocket – allowing Cathy to see them as she walked around the nursing home. According to Cathy, it was an attempt to intimidate her, and it worked. She said she was, at that point, terrified of her lover.

"I was afraid that something would happen to me," Cathy said.

Detectives weren't sure what to believe. According to Tom, Cathy was refusing to take any responsibility for the murders – and she'd managed to convince him that she was telling the truth. Roger, though, had his doubts.

"I thought she was manipulative," Roger said. "Tom, on the other hand, was trying to fit all these pieces together and I just kept thinking that she's not telling the whole truth, she may have an ulterior motive here."

Cathy agreed to take a polygraph test to support her story, which immediately backfired – the operator was confident that Cathy's account was completely made up. But detectives decided the only way to be sure was to talk to Gwen Graham.

"I ended up flying down to Tyler, Texas, where I met the investigator down there," said Roger.

A search warrant is obtained for Gwen's home, owing to her outstanding warrant. When detectives show up at the house, they are greeted by Gwen and her new live-in girlfriend. According to Roger, Gwen was "mild and polite."

"She didn't seem like the person that everybody was saying she was," he said.

While officers execute the search warrant in Gwen's home, she is taken to the police station for further questioning. Nothing is found at her home that could tie her to the series of deaths at the Michigan nursing home – and during her interview with detectives, Gwen denies any knowledge of murder.

"I was not present at the time of any of these people's deaths. I was somewhere in the building, working – that's all I know," she said. "Cathy's a sick mind, she'd say anything."

When police inquired about Gwen and Cathy's relationship, Gwen told them that at first, things were great – but then, the relationship took on a darker edge. Gwen admitted she was growing frustrated with Cathy's insatiable desire to manipulate others.

"I got tired of her playing games, all the games that were going on with people's heads," she said.

She described one incident where, for Halloween, she was dressed up as a patient. According to Gwen's story, Cathy used the medical restraints that were a part of Gwen's costume to tie her down to the bed. This led to increasingly violent sexual play, Gwen said, until Cathy became physically abusive and dominating.

In an attempt to end the relationship, Gwen started a secret affair with another nurses' aide at Alpine Manor. She said when she finally left Cathy, she began fearing for her life.

"Cathy threatens Gwen's new girlfriend, saying, 'you know, I can put Gwen away for a long, long time in prison,'" explained Cauffiel.

According to Cauffiel, Gwen's mounting concern led her to move back in with Cathy – but the stay was short-lived. During that brief time, Gwen said Cathy tied her up, took her gun, and began threatening her.

"I was begging, because I thought she was going to shoot me, and then she just looked at me real strange and she left, she left the house," Gwen said, adding that she eventually managed to escape by returning to Texas.

She also maintained her denial that any murders took place while she was working at Alpine Manor – asserting that Cathy was just upset about the break up. Gwen agreed to a polygraph test, which returned inconclusive results.

The Michigan detectives were forced to leave Texas without the evidence they were hoping to find. While most investigators were ready to put the case to rest, Tom Freeman was unable to shake the feeling that something awful occurred at the nursing home.

"In the world that Gwen and Cathy exist in, they were perfectly matched because what the other one lacked, her partner fulfilled," Palmatier said. "So, when you put these two chemicals, these two things together, it created an explosion – and in any explosion, people die."

On October 17, 1988, Tom sat down with Cathy to discuss her failed polygraph. He told her that the reason he believes she was lying is that she wasn't just Gwen Graham's lookout – instead, he thinks Cathy actually participated in the murders. But Cathy didn't respond. She left the interview without a word, but called back just three days later and said she was finally ready to talk about the killings.

This time, Cathy admitted that she planned the whole thing together with Gwen. According to Cathy, the patients were killed as part of a game she and Gwen had invented called "The Murder Game." She explained to Tom that the point of the game was to select and kill each patient in a particular order, using the first initial of each victim's name to spell the word "MURDER."

"The problem with spelling out the word 'MURDER' as the homicides occurred, was that there were several patients that were very active and struggled, and they couldn't actually kill them," Tom said. "So, the game itself, to spell out the word, never got finished – they got to a point where it was the easiest patient to kill."

Investigators were unconvinced – according to Abramsky, Gwen's personality disorder would likely have prevented her from hatching such an elaborate, sophisticated plot. Instead, he said, the game seemed much more Cathy's style.

"Gwen is easily influenced by others for several reasons. One, she doesn't have a stable self-identity, which says this is right and this is wrong, so she's very, very malleable in that particular sense," said Abramsky. "The other thing is that she's subject to thrills and impulse behaviour, so when people suggest things, she doesn't have that barrier that says, 'wait a second, that's the wrong thing to do.'"

Every time Cathy and Gwen killed a patient together, she said, their relationship became more intense. They were growing closer and closer together – often expressing their love for one another through the use of a favorite phrase, which they began altering with each successful kill.

"They'd say, 'I love you forever,' and then it became 'I love you forever and a day,' and then it became 'forever and two days,' and supposedly, each day represented a murder," Cauffiel said. "So, after five murders, it was, 'I love you forever and five days,' and that was symbolic of the murderous bond they had together."

However, Cathy told police that eventually, the game became too much for her to handle. She hadn't actually killed anyone herself, she explained – she was just acting as a lookout for Gwen because she loved her so much, and she wanted Gwen to love her back. She said she was willing to participate as a lookout, but once Gwen decided it was Cathy's turn to hold the washcloth, she refused.

And, when police questioned Cathy during a polygraph test, the results indicated that this time, her story was factually true.

"I think we're dealing with highly disturbed people – and their motivations are not the same motivations that make most people tick," said Abramsky.

"I thought it was a joke."

In January of 1989, Judge Sherwin Venema ordered Cathy to stand trial for two of the deaths the pair was suspected to have committed. The preliminary hearing lasted four hours, and included testimony provided by three witnesses claiming that Cathy and Gwen had killed the patients together.

The first witness was Ken Wood, Cathy's ex-husband, who said Cathy had told him that she and Gwen had committed the murders "just because it was fun." The other two witnesses were former nurses' aides who had worked at Alpine Manor with Gwen and Cathy, and each relayed similar stories while on the stand.

According to Russell Thatcher, who spent six months working at the nursing home in 1987, said that when he asked Cathy why they had killed the patients, she replied that it was "just to relieve Gwen's stress if she was having a bad day."

Although Dawn Male had been let go in 1986, before the murders occurred, she heard about them directly from Gwen and Cathy while she was visiting them at the home they had shared in Grand Rapids.

"I didn't believe them," she said. "I thought it was a joke – a sick joke, but a joke. Head games."

The women were known for telling outrageous stories to try and mess with people, she told the court, noting that it was Cathy who had a particular knack for it.

But it was Gwen who was the violent one, she claimed – adding that at one point, Gwen "beat the crap out of me."

A friend of Cathy's, Nancy Harris, said Cathy had told her about the murders, but said she only witnessed them – she hadn't participated or reported it. According to Nancy, Cathy was "afraid for her life," and that Gwen was "capable of killing anyone."

According to Venema, it was "clear and concise that two deaths occurred as the result of criminal agency," adding there was enough evidence for Cathy to stand trial.

During the trial, Cathy managed to plea bargain her way to a reduced sentence – alleging to the court that the entire thing was Gwen's idea, while she served only as a lookout. She was charged with just one count of second-degree murder and one count of conspiracy to commit second-degree murder. Cathy was sentenced to twenty years for each charge, and will likely be released in 2021.

Gwen Graham, who maintained her innocence throughout the trial and claimed the entire story was one of Cathy's "mind games," was found guilty of five counts of murder and one count of conspiracy to commit murder. She received five life sentences.

KILL THEM CHELSEA

Samantha Reed

There are many motives for murder whether it is revenge, love, or money. Sometimes people just kill other people for the sheer pleasure of it, according to their statements when they are caught. It is the ones that kill for money that often have the most intricate conspiracies attached to them, the most 'flawless' of plans, and they are also the ones that often find themselves caught. This is a story of love, money, conspiracy, and murder out of Mansfield, Texas. It is a murder that made headlines of Tarrant County and one people will not be quick to forget.

In The Beginning

Chelsea Lea Richardson was born March 26 1984. She came from a regular working class family and grew up in a working class neighbourhood in Tarrant County, Texas. She had a regular childhood if one that was a little strained. Her father, an ironworker and former marine, had died young and her mother had worked constantly to make ends meet for the two children.

Chelsea was a social person. She would go to the IHOP with her brother and sit for hours while he played Yu-Gi-Oh with his friends. She would chat and waste away the hours. She had never cared for the card game, but being at the IHOP was better than being at home. And it was through this connection that she first met Andrew Wamsley.

Andrew Wamsley was born July 7, 1984 and was the second child of Rick and Suzanna Wamsley, a wealthy, upper class family in Tarrant County, Texas. He'd had a life with every comfort possible. It was a life that was a great contrast to the one Chelsea had lived and perhaps that was what drew her to him. His parents had been strict, but they had ensured that their entire world revolved around their children. And in doing so, they had isolated them from the world, from people outside of their high-class social group, and from those that they didn't approve of.

Chelsea and Andrew began a relationship in January 2003 despite their differences, or perhaps because of them. They began to spend a great deal of time out at Ruth Brustrom's house. Ruth, whose husband had been like a second father to Chelsea, was glad to have the company. She said, "Andrew seemed like a real sweet kid. The best guy she'd brought out here. He seemed real honest."

They liked the laid-back atmosphere out at the Brustrom place. There was no need to be anything other than what they wanted to be out there. It was a nice, secluded piece of country property filled with possibilities.

Still, reality can't sit in the background forever. Chelsea, without the wealth behind her and luxury that Andrew has, needs to look for a job and consider her future. However, she shows no real ambition towards going through with any sort of career options. Andrew is equally unambitious. Despite being enrolled in college, he rarely attended classes.

Chelsea and Andrew were looking for simple solutions in life. For Andrew, perhaps it was because everything had always been handed to him. For Chelsea, perhaps it was because she had struggled for everything in her life already and she was desperate for a break. Regardless of the reason, the need to cut corners appeared early in their relationship.

Not As They Appear

Families that have a great deal of money and status tend to also have a great deal of familial issues; they just are better at sweeping them under the rug than the rest of the world. The Wamsley's were no exception to this rule. And their greatest issues came from their eldest child, Sarah Wamsley.

The family harboured a deep suspicion of people outside of their social circle and this is a belief that they worked hard to instill in their children. The mother, Suzy Wamsley, was raised in the Church of Christ but she carried none of the religious moorings with her into her family life despite taking all of the religious structure with her.

She taught her children to believe that "people were only nice to them for their own reasons". And this continued the suspicious nature. Sarah suffered more at the hands of this rhetoric than Andrew, and the outcomes were detrimental to her overall growth as an individual.

The Wamsley's had constant problems with their daughter Sarah. They considered her to be a rebellious teen and were always seeking a solution to this issue. If they could find a pill to fix her they would, but it seemed that her problems were there to stay.

Andrew admitted to fighting constantly with his sister and not having a stable relationship with his parents in one of his many conversations with Ruth Brustrom. His parents sent Sarah to a psychiatric facility when she was sixteen in hopes of dealing with the "problem" that was her rebellious nature.

Sarah was diagnosed with bipolar disorder and weeks before Sarah was to graduate high school, the Wamsley's kicked her out of the house. They tossed her belongings on the front lawn and left her on her own. They'd had enough of her "rebellion" and enough of her "mood swings". This was in 1997.

Sarah's life didn't improve from that point on. She had a child with the man she moved in with after her parent's kicked her out. She lost custody of her daughter and went into a depressive spiral where she even tried to kill herself. She now lives with her paternal grandparents in Oklahoma.

Andrew continued to have a strained relationship with his parents, particularly his father. Friends of the family said that Andrew was a spoiled, immature, and impulsive child. They had quite often witness instances where Andrew had displayed violent behaviour or outbursts that seemed quite irrational.

Andrew would quite often say that he hated his father and that he didn't agree with the way his father wanted him to live his life. With one child having so obviously failed the family, it was not surprising that the Wamsley's would put pressure on Andrew to make better choices. But they had raised him to be entitled and they were reaping the outcomes of that.

Friends and family weren't the only ones to think that Andrew was a little high on himself. His co-workers at the Putt-Putt Golf also found him arrogant and entitled. Many would go as far as not wanting to work a shift with him. He quit before he would be fired from the position.

In the fall of 2003 Andrew dropped out of college and as result his parents cut him off financially. Without a job or a place to live, Andrew found himself living almost full time with the Richardsons. Their living situation was far from what Andrew was used to. It was described as being "filthy, with roaches crawling on the ceiling".

Soon after the Richardsons got another housemate with Susana Toledano. She moved in after having a conflict with her mother. It appeared as though the Richardson household was becoming the safe house for those with family troubles. It was a group of young adults with no purpose and no ambition all group under one roof. It was a combination that was doomed to fail.

Everyone Has a Purpose

Susana Toledano and Chelsea had been friends for several years now. Susana was struggling to make her way through high school and work a part time job at the same time. In Susana, perhaps, Chelsea saw the opportunity to have influence over someone in her life. Susana was a girl with low self-esteem and she was eager to please. She would do whatever Chelsea wanted her to do, and therein lie her purpose.

Andrew saw in Chelsea an opportunity. Whether he originally intended to use her as a scapegoat or just wanted someone else to do the dirty work it is hard to say. It was clear that he never intended on cutting her in on the end goal. Andrew was too selfish for something like that.

It was in October 2003 when they began to plot the murder of his parents. And naturally, the trio met at the IHOP to discuss their plot.

Their choice of public location would backfire on them, but that was something they clearly had no intent to consider.

It began as conversations of events that would require minimal amounts of effort on their behalf. They could cut the break lines in the family vehicle and it would be written off as an accident. However, the conversation wasn't just about Rick and Suzy Wamsley, it was about Sarah too. No Wamsley could remain other than Andrew otherwise it would ruin the entire plan.

A decision was made about how things would be handled when Andrew asked Hilario Cardenas, a manager at the IHOP, to get him a gun. The method had been chosen and now it was just a matter of going through with the plan.

Attempt Number One

Andrew was growing tired of scrapping by and living off of what he could make at a part time job, if he was lucky enough to keep one. He knew that there was easy money to be made if only he could get his family out of the way. He was set to inherit $1 million if only he could find a way to get them out of the picture.

He tried to sabotage their car first. But it seemed that the group of them weren't very good at taking that route. They had a few failed attempts before Andrew asked Hilario to get him a gun and he pursued a more direct method of contact.

Still, this didn't work out well in the favour of the group of conspirators. On November 9, 2003 at 2:30pm the Wamsley's were driving down Interstate 35 when they heard a loud thud on their car. When they pulled into Chili's for dinner, they found a bulled hole in the rear panel of their Jeep Laredo.

Suzy Wamsley immediately called Andrew and demanded to know where he was. Rick Wamsley called the police and filed a formal report about the incident. Beyond that point, despite Sarah insisting on wanting to talk further about it, they spoke no more on the matter.

The group of conspirators had been functioning under the belief that if they shot at the gas tank they could make the car explode. The three of them had been in Andrew's Mustang when the shots were fired. Susana had taken the shots and Andrew was very angry with her for missing the shot.

Despite having practiced with the handgun out at the Brustrom property and being the second best shot, Susana had still failed in her attempt to make the car explode. It was time to step things up. There would be no mistakes the second time around. Andrew wanted this done and he was going to make sure that it happened.

The Final Attempt

It was a month later before things escalated to their final scene. On December 11, 2003 at 11:40pm 911 received a call from the Wamsley residence but no one spoke on the phone. The police arrived at the house four minutes later to find the garage door open and the door from the garage to the house also open.

They found Suzy Wamsley on the living room couch. She had been shot in the left ear with a large caliber weapon and had been stabled a minimum of eighteen times in the neck and chest. The violence associated with that action alone was shocking.

They found Rick Wamsley in his boxer shorts. He had been shot in the face and the back and also had been stabbed multiple times. There was clearly something personal about this crime. There was clearly anger and emotion attached to this action.

The police found bloody footprints throughout the living room, dining room, and entryway. There was no indication of forced entry into the house and there were no signs of robbery.

The neighbourhood where the Wamsley's lived took the news of their murder with the expected level of fear and suspicion. Was there a robber on the loose? Had they been killed for money? Where would they strike next?

The police did everything they could to shut down suspicions surrounding the case. They assured the community that it was an isolated crime and that there was no risk to the rest of the community.

But gossip will always run wild in gated communities. The residents of Walnut Estates came up with many possible theories on what had happened to the Wamsley's. Each one was more far-fetched than the one before it. The truth behind what had happened was one none of them had considered and one that would give them something to talk about for years to come.

Suspects and Arrests

Originally the police took interest in Todd Cleveland due to the particularly bitter custody battle between him and Sarah over their child. However, Todd cleared a polygraph test and was released from custody.

The Wamsley children were target next as potential suspects as they had the most to gain, financially, from their parents' death. They each had claim to over $100 000 in cash and a $1 million life insurance policy. Those were very persuasive numbers, especially considering the position that both the children were in.

Andrew and Chelsea went willingly to the police station on December 12, 2003. They claimed to have been at the Richardson's house since their visit with the Wamsley's on December 9th. They had originally intented on going camping, but the colder weather had led them to seek a weekend spent indoors.

Andrew had initially agreed to let the police search his car, but quickly withdrew this consent. This led to the Mustang being impounded and the police searching it from that point. They found traces of human blood in the back passenger seat and two front seats. There was evidence that a large amount of blood had been in the car at one point in time, but it had thoroughly been cleaned and no DNA evidence could be taken from it.

Both Wamsley children agreed to take polygraph tests. Sarah passed and Andrew failed. Chelsea and Andrew refused to provide DNA samples and at that point the cooperation was over.

In January the police subpoenaed eight people to provide DNA samples, including Andrew, Chelsea, Sarah, and Susana. Susana was included because she was Chelsea's roommate and also had dyed hair. They were looking to match the DNA with strands found in Rick Wamsley's hand.

Andrew and Chelsea took refuge at the Brustrom property after the initial investigation began. However, tensions between the couple grew. Andrew would get stressed and grow quiet. Chelsea would cry. And when they fought it was violent.

Eventually they went back to the Richardson's house in early March. Perhaps they thought the investigation would have calmed down by then and it was safe to go back to town. But things were just beginning.

Meanwhile, Sarah was doing whatever she could to block Andrew's attempts to collect on his parent's life insurance policy. Despite denying any connection to the murders she was adamant on blocking his access to the money until the investigation was over. And considering the fact that he was still considered a suspect in their murders, her filed claim was passed and it was deemed that Andrew was to benefit in no way from the death of his parents at the time being.

DMA evidence didn't come back until March 30, 2004 and it identified Susana Toledano as a perfect match. At that point in time she had disappeared from Tarrant County and was found by police in Addison, Illinois. She was arrest on April 4th and her statements led the police to the IHOP and Hilario Cardenas who had not been under investigation up until that point. Andrew and Chelsea were arrested on April 7th. All four have been in prison since.

Murder and Sentencing

During the trial the truth of what happened on the day of December 11th was revealed.

They entered the Wamsley house that evening and Chelsea coached Susana through how to carry out the shootings. After the talk, Susana shot Suzy Wamsley in the head while she slept on the living room couch. She died instantly from the wound.

Rick Wamsley was not such an easy victim. He'd been awakened by the sound of the shooting. Susana went to the master bedroom to shoot Rick but he charged her as she came into the bedroom. The bullet struck him just above the eyebrow, but he still managed to tackle Susana to the ground and knock the gun out of her hand. Chelsea picked the gun up and shot Rick in the back to make him get off of Susana.

Now they ran into the problem that there were no more bullets in the gun and neither of them was certain if the Wamsley's were actually dead. Chelsea's solution to this was to grab two large kitchen knives. Meanwhile, Andrew struggled with his father in the entryway. Chelsea stabbed him in the back repeatedly until he stopped moving. She then ordered Susana to return to the living room and stab Suzy to ensure that she was dead.

They fled in Andrew's Mustang after discarding their outwear in a garbage bag that Chelsea had brought along. They cleaned and detailed Andrew's car in order to remove all of the blood from it. And then they went back to their routines.

"It was an incredibly brutal and frightening crime scene," Page Simpson, a Tarrant County prosecutor said.

Chelsea had manipulated a mentally challenged nineteen-year-old to create a false alibi for them in order to protect them from the events of that evening. She had befriended the boy, Jeremy Lavender, and convinced him that he was her boyfriend. However, when questioned by police he quickly admitted that the alibi was false.

Chelsea, Andrew, and Susana were called before a grand jury.

Chelsea was sentenced with a charge of capital murder in less than three hours.

Susana, who had entered a plea bargain in exchange for her cooperation with the State, was charged with life in prison for murder. She will not be up for parole for thirty years.

And Andrew was convicted of capital murder in his 2005 trial.

Chelsea Richardson was the first person to be sentenced to death in Tarrant County. This sentence did not last long.

Her trial was appealed and due to misconduct by the prosecutor of the first trial and withholding evidence from the defence, the sentence was reduced. Chelsea will serve forty years in prison before she is eligible for parole.

The defence wanted her to achieve the impossible. They wanted her to walk away free of all charges, but that outcome was not possible considering the mountain of evidence against her. Instead, all the defence could accomplish was to get her off of death row. For now, that would have to be enough.

Although there is talk of fighting for all of the incarcerated members to be released on earlier parole dates than originally mandated, the potential for this to happen seems to be limited. The State of Texas seems fairly firm on where it stands on keeping the co-conspirators in prison for the horrendous murders of Suzy and Rick Wamsley. It is not something that will be quickly forgotten.

The Careful Wrath of Michelle Reynolds

The city of Rome, Georgia, nestled in the foothills of the Appalachian mountains and occupying the administrative center of Floyd County, is not known for its production of nation-wide news. Indeed, to the outside observer, the city (home to 36,000) would likely appear as nondescript as any mid-sized, somewhat detached American city would be. As the nation would discover in mid-2004, however; even places like Rome can produce a scene of such horror as to grip a country by the hair, gluing its citizens to their TV screens.

On the morning of July 5, 2004, an employee of Rome's Frito-Lay distribution center was pulling into work when he noticed a man standing by the doorway. The employee initially thought nothing of the stranger, since workers commonly arrived at the center during dawn hours. After a moment, however, it became clear that the man standing by the doorway was visibly nervous, and he made a hasty exit. Naturally, the witness entered the building to see what the stranger had been up to. What he found was the body of Thad John Glenn Reynolds, 36 years old. He was stabbed a total of 19 times and was left for dead.

The ensuing media coverage and police investigation shook Rome to its core. Thad John Glenn Reynolds, Frito-Lay's district manager for the Rome/Cartersville area was, by virtually all accounts, an inordinately kind-hearted, gentle, caring person, who also happened to serve as church deacon. It was natural for anyone following the story to question motive, and of course to convey their sympathies to the victim's family members. That's where things take a turn deeper into the dark.

As has since been concluded by the Georgia Supreme Court, the murder was a premeditated operation executed by Reynolds' wife's lover, Richard Scott Harper (who, with his own wife, also happened to be close friends with the Reynolds), and Reynolds' wife herself,

Michelle. As far as sensational media coverage goes, there are few things as dramatic and obscene as a wife and her lover conspiring to kill her husband. Understandably, the media locked its attention on the criminal duo, with a honed focus on Michelle.

Michelle Reynolds, born Michelle Sullins, spent her childhood pining for the spotlight, as her aunt Trish Benefield tells NBC correspondent Dennis Murphy. "She was always wanting to pose for my camera," Benefield reflects. "And she would sit at my mom's and dad's in the swing, I would take her picture. So grab the little poodle, you know, the doggy, and take another picture."

What wasn't so apparent in the smile Michelle always brought to her family photographs was the considerable strife she endured throughout her childhood. After coping with the separation of her parents in the earliest days of her youth, Michelle suffered the death of her father, who passed away when she was 13 years old. Lacking any other option, her mother took the reigns of the family into her own hands, submerging Michelle and her two brothers in the moral teachings of the Baptist Church.

Michelle adapted to the loss of her father as best she could, adjusting to her new life in uneventful Rome. As she grew older, there was no denying how strikingly attractive she was becoming, and her potential suitors were quick to notice.

"I mean, she was just a beauty, absolutely," says Benefield. "Walk into a room, and everybody looks. You know, she had that presence."

When Michelle is asked by Murphy if she was "the really cool girl at school," she responds with, "I guess."

A cool and quiet girl, but perhaps not quite as reserved as she might seem, Michelle humored her potential suitors throughout her high school years, cycling through a few boyfriends before one fateful encounter at a football game.

As with any high school sporting event, energies were high. Indeed, much of the energy of the night was coming from Michelle's corner, care of her and her fellow cheerleaders. One of the players from the opposing team - carrying the number 15 on his jersey - caught her attention. The teenager was a young Thad Reynolds, and he was quick to return the beautiful cheerleader's gaze right back to her.

A lifelong native of Rome, Thad Reynolds was uncommonly active during his high school years, serving as a member of the Coosa High School wrestling team as well as its football team. Before the night of the football game, and for the rest of his life after, Thad Reynolds was almost unanimously described by his friends and family as generous, caring, and lovingly involved. His aura that night turned out to be more than enough to attract the prettiest cheerleader on the field. As the reports go, when Thad and Michelle locked eyes for the first time, the rest was history.

Beverly Owens, Thad's sister, recalls their meeting. "He was the football player. She was the cheerleader. I mean, I guess that's how it started," she explains to Murphy.

"A lot of people called us 'Ken' and 'Barbie,'" Michelle says to Murphy.

No aspect of the pair's courtship could have foreshadowed the horror lurking ahead. In fact, their first date was virtually as simple as it could get - a tractor pull in Atlanta with Thad's family. During her blooming teenage romance, Michelle, like most teenagers her age, was overtaken by butterflies. "And actually when we got back to their house, I got sick and threw up because I was so nervous," she says.

If ever a dark omen of their relationship did manifest itself during that time, it came two months after they began dating In a swooping romantic gesture, Thad asked Michelle to wear his class ring. Ten minutes after she put it on (the exact date was January 28th, 1986), the U.S. space shuttle exploded. Despite being taken by the news, neither Thad nor Michelle considered this to be a bad sign. Their relationship progressed naturally from that point forward.

Thad and Michelle went to prom together. They graduated, celebrated, and got married without much delay. 15 now being their signature number, the couple chose to get married on August the 15th at Hollywood Baptist, the church that would play such a prominent role in the couple's married lives during the years to come.

Naturally, friends and family of the couple were delighted about their reunion. "This was it. This was her family. She was finally going to have what she wanted," Ms. Benefield tells Murphy.

During its early days, the marriage seemed not to disappoint Michelle, either. When Murphy asked her how it felt to be a married woman, Michelle replied, "It was awesome. I enjoyed it. And having our own place was nice." She was happy, living with the man she loved and knowing that, unlike the father who abandoned her before passing away, her husband was reliable, and was sure to stick around until death did them part.

Michelle's aunt, noting her niece's relationship from a distance, also had faith in Thad. The young man was kind and clear-headed, and everyone who knew him would vouch for him. Ms. Benefield would look at Thad and see a safe, loving future ahead for her niece. "... because when I saw them together I saw that. I saw that security. I know she loved him. I also know that she could lean on him and depend on him."

Like any young couple freshly married, Thad and Michelle had plans of a bright future ahead of them. "We had goals," Michelle recalls. "We wanted to buy a house, we wanted to go on a cruise and buy a camcorder; and we did all three. And after that, we decided to try and start having children."

They succeeded, and Michelle gave birth to a little girl named Olivia. Judging by appearances, it would seem that the couple was on their way to settling down just as they planned to. However, as time went on, their relationship was beginning to buckle under pressure. After fighting to stay together seemed to prove fruitless, Michelle and Thad divorced five years into their marriage.

When asked about this period, Michelle puts things simply: "We had problems."

"One had cheated. The other one had cheated," explains Benefield. "So you have both stories."

The two coped with the divorce as best they could, with Thad seeming to take is the hardest. While Michelle attempted to settle into her new life by starting a new job at an office and dating every so often, Thad was having trouble getting back on his feet. His mother, Kitty Walker, recalls a night when her son, in a state of total despair, gave her a call.

"He was in an apartment that he had rented, and I can remember him saying that he curled up in the fetal position in the closet and asked for God and asked for reconciliation."

While Michelle wasn't having as trying a time as Thad, she doesn't recall finding much satisfaction through dating as a single mom. "I dated a few times, but I knew back in my mind that I still loved Thad, and I kept our wedding rings in our safe. But we still did things together. We had Christmas together and some holidays, and I even went to Florida with his family. So it's almost like we really wasn't divorced."

Four years passed this way, with the couple making a pseudo effort to establish themselves on their own while still remaining tied to each other socially. After a while, it became clear to both Thad and Michelle that whatever love they had for each other was still there in some way. They went into counselling, and emerged fully reconciled. They got remarried at the same church, renewing their vows to start fresh.

Thad was newly invigorated by the reunion with his wife, committing himself to forming a tight-knit family. They would eventually have three more girls, and the Hollywood Baptist Church would serve as their family's foundation. The Reynolds', as a unit, loved their simple, happy lifestyle, and they enjoyed the church network they were a part of. As it happened, another couple, bearing several similarities to Thad and Michelle, were also part of that network: Scotty and Paige Harper.

When Murphy asks Scotty about Thad during their interview, he replies simply, "You know, he was—he was a good guy."

After meeting the first few times, it became clear that the couples would become best of friends. Thad and Scotty had so much in common, after all. Murphy goes over their similarities: "Like Thad and Michelle, they lived next door to his parents. Like Thad, Scotty was deeply religious and also a church volunteer leader. He was the volunteer family pastor, giving his time to tend to the young people of Hollywood Baptist. And Scotty and Paige had their own three small children, also all girls."

On Thad's end, there was clear admiration and respect for Scotty. On stage one night at the Hollywood Baptist Church, Thad said to the assembly, "Our family pastor, official title now, Scotty Harper, has always taught the people that are under him and the kids that we need to teach them the things that are relevant to them these days. That's his keyword, right? Relevant. How to minister to them right now with their lives."

Meanwhile, on the wives' end, it soon became clear that the same close bond would not be formed between Michelle and Paige. According to Michelle: "Scotty told me later on that she was jealous of me and asking him if he thought she was prettier than me, and she was just jealous of me, and so she just started getting away from me."

While she didn't see much potential in forming a connection with Paige, Michelle made no effort to prevent her from getting closer to Scotty. Indeed, Michelle would see Scotty almost every day, since he was directing the performances her teenagers were meant to give for the church.

In 2004, Michelle was evidently yearning for something other than her life in Rome, Georgia, tied so strongly to the church and its community. She was dreaming of a different setting, specifically in the

Smoky Mountains, Tennessee. Loving her dearly, Thad followed his wife down this new exploration, and they eventually found a cabin that they thought had potential. They pursued the investment and qualified for financing. However, before being able to finalize, they were edged out by another buyer. According to Thad, this incident sparked a long depression in his wife.

Michelle began neglecting her family duties over the coming months, not making the effort to visit her in-laws - who lived next door - as often as she used to.

Murphy summarizes the couple's relationship during this time: "When Thad got home from work, she'd say she'd had a long day with the kids and she was going off to shop. Thad, meanwhile, was becoming even more involved in the church. After a missionary trip to Cuba, he came back home afire with the idea of becoming a minister full-time, leaving his job to see where Jesus would lead him. Michelle was said to be frosty to the idea. When did it begin? We'll never know, but Michelle, feeling she was playing second fiddle to God in her marriage, began telling someone she was having naughty thoughts about him. Someone very taboo. And he was only too happy to say, 'Funny, me, too.'"

According to Michelle, the forbidden romance between her and Scotty bloomed gradually, beginning with small flirtations that grew increasingly obvious. One day, Michelle met Scotty at work, and they consummated their affair in the backseat of Scotty's car.

The two were good at keeping their affair a secret, though Scotty was concerned that his wife would leave him. Michelle, meanwhile, seemed to be certain that she would not be getting divorced from Thad. However, the couple would joke in dark ways with each other when they were alone. In one instance, Michelle said, "If you want me as your bride, then you're just going to have to outlive Thad."

When asked about this, Scotty says, "Maybe it did put some things in my head."

As time went on, the two spoke increasingly often about a potential meeting between Thad and Scotty. Their code word for describing this hypothetical meeting was "ugly", meaning that's how things would get should the two ever meet to have "the talk." Moreover, this is where Michelle's suspicious behavior begins, as she starts to tell Scotty about certain places where her husband likes to go when he's alone. Reportedly, Michelle would send messages to Scotty during this time which read like, "Have you talked to him yet? Have you done the thing you promised you were going to do?"

When asked about this, Michelle told Murphy, "I just asked him when he was going to talk to him."

On July 1st, Scotty purchased a knife from Kmart, and what he intended to use it for was clear. However, that same day, he grew cold feet. When expressing this to Michelle, she did nothing to pedal things back. Instead, she told Scotty, "You're not man enough to do this thing you said you were going to do?" and "And forget about me, bud, because I'm going to be gone."

According to Murphy, "...Scotty received an e-mail from Michelle with information about where Thad was going to be the next morning, Monday. After the chilly talk at the levee, Scotty new full well that he might lose Michelle unless he confronted Thad soon, even if it turned out to be that lovers' shorthand they had, 'ugly.' And ugly it would be, after a bloody, predawn discovery."

All of which lead, ultimately, to the murder of Thad John Glenn Reynolds in the Rome Frito-Lay warehouse. The words that Scotty reportedly spoke to Thad during this encounter have now become infamous: "I want what you got."

The town was shaken. "We typically have maybe two murders a year," says Rome sheriff Burkhalter. "This kind of gruesome murder was, of course, very eye-opening for our community and very big news."

One local said, "No one could make sense of it. It just seemed out of character for what is a nice, quiet place to live."

Michelle played the role of devastated widow quite well, reacting precisely as friends and family would expect her to. However, it soon became clear that she would not get away from the incident scot-free. As Murphy explains: "Scotty, out of sight overnight in a psych ward, was also buying Michelle the time she wanted to prepare for Thad's funeral without the pall of Scotty's involvement hanging over it. But no one in their circle suspected yet that Scotty Harper could be the killer. Friends were nonetheless privately buzzing about the new widow's demeanor. Why did Michelle seem so calm? And why did she tell the ladies who asked if they could help her shop for a funeral dress that that wouldn't be necessary? She had a new black dress in her closet with the price tag still on it. What was going on with the newly widowed Michelle?"

Thankfully, the Rome police force was efficient in its investigation. Three days following the murder, Michelle and Scotty were officially charged. Harper was immediately deemed the executioner who carried out the murder, while Michelle was accused of assisting the murder by helping Scotty plan an attack.

While they made quick work of the case, Murphy explains that the duo didn't exactly make the task impossible for the police force. "Even an armchair detective would have started following the trail right to Scotty Harper's door. The killer had used a knife like this to stab Thad Reynolds 19 times that Monday morning. The detectives knew that on the morning of the murder Scotty Harper had gone to the ER of the hospital where he worked to have a cut hand stitched up. Those explicit e-mails he failed to get rid of told them he was a month into an affair with the murdered man's wife. Had Scotty Harper murdered his best friend, the husband of his lover?"

The media response was instant. As mentioned, there are few news stories as sensational as a supposedly loving wife plotting with her lover to kill her husband. According to the Rome News-Tribune, in their one-year followup to the incident: "Both Scott Harper and Michelle

Reynolds face five counts of murder, two counts of aggravated assault — one for aggravated assault with intent to murder and one for aggravated assault with a deadly weapon — one count of aggravated battery and one count of burglary in relation to the incident." Additionally, Scott Harper was charged with possession of a deadly weapon.

Over the next few years, the prosecution for the conspiring murderers was being arranged. During that time, Michelle and Scotty were detained in prison.

The next update of the case came in 2008, when Scotty officially pleaded guilty to the 2004 murder. Scotty and the state agreed that, should Scotty testify against Michelle, the state would not aim for a death penalty against her.

The case was finally shut in January 2010. John Bailey of the Rome News-Tribune reported: "More than five years after the murder of Thad John Glenn Reynolds — just two weeks prior to the scheduled beginning of a trial — Michelle Reynolds took a plea deal and agreed to be sentenced to 20 years in prison Wednesday and Scott Harper will begin to serve the rest of his natural life in a state penitentiary."

On the side of the bereaved, justice was not the biggest priority. All Thad's mother wanted to ensure was that the four Reynolds daughters would be protected from the reach of their mother.

During his sentencing, when Harper was offered the opportunity to address the court. "There's nothing I can say to undo what was done," he said through tears, calling his actions selfish and foolish. He then apologized to his ex-wife and three daughters, saying, "I'm ashamed of the things I thought and did in 2004."

Understandably, those observing the case did not accept Scotty's regret with open arms, claiming that the tears he shed were "alligator tears". To this, Scotty's attorney objected. "He cries those tears when nobody is looking ... He cries those tears when he's alone in his cell, and he cries those tears in the morning and at night," Adams told the court.

Michelle, meanwhile, showed no discernible sign of emotion during her testimony and sentencing.

Of course, the day would not be complete without some kind of confrontation in the courtroom. Thad's mother Kitty could not stomach seeing her ex daighter-in-law behave so robotically after having her son murdered. In a fit of emotion, Kitty famously asked Michelle, "Why? Why not just walk away?" After more than five years had passed since her son's death, this was all she wanted to know.

Michelle, who for that entire court day uttered little other than "yes, sir," when speaking to the judge, did not formulate a response to Kitty's question. All she did was stare blankly, in no direction in particular, with no discernible facial expression. Actually, she offered one clear gesture to the courtroom before being handcuffed: laughter. As the bailiff escorted her out of the courtroom, Michelle let one small laugh escape her lips.

More than five years after the murder, Thad's family and the town of Rome finally saw its justice. Michelle Reynolds and Scotty Harper were headed to prison.

Following their imprisonment, there was some sparse media follow-up to the Reynolds' case. There were limitations put on how often Michelle could see her daughters, to which the mother objected publicly and in writing. As it stands, the judge concluded that the children could only visit their mother when they reach adulthood.

Michelle's tactics as an accomplice in this murder, though despicable, should be noted as effective, at least for a while. One can assume that she spent a lot of time analyzing the case from the perspective of the police. She was extremely careful to avoid saying or doing anything incriminating. Murphy on Michelle's reservedness as an accomplice: "Not in any of the recovered e-mails had Michelle written words to the effect, 'We need to kill Thad.' So instead the prosecutors focused on that Fourth of July weekend that began with that frosty rendezvous at the levee on Friday. By that day, Scotty had already failed on two occasions to confront Thad after he says Michelle had given him instructions as to where he would be. To Scotty she seemed upset that afternoon that he hadn't been manly enough to tell Thad. He thought he'd lost her. Sunday she e-mails Scotty, letting him know where Thad will be early the next morning."

So, what this case presents is a classic archetype: the conniving trickster whispering evils into the ears of a willing, strong instrument. Without the instrument, there would only be whispers; without the whispers, there would be no murder. It was rotten luck for a good man that brought the two together in the first place.

It would take a psychologist to analyze Michelle's pathology, so there's no use attempting to go deeply into it here. Suffice it to say that, taking her actions in this case at face value, Michelle wanted her husband dead, and she knew that Scotty was the ideal man to get the job done. So it goes.

Meanwhile, in Rome, life resumes. Kitty still sits in the same spot on the church bench, and her granddaughters sit next to her. The rolling Appalachians shelter the town, as they always have. Whether Rome will ever see another homicide the likes of which was produced here, no one can say. What is clear is that, in this case at least, justice was served in full force. The people of Rome can sleep freely knowing that Michelle Reynolds and her wrath are safely behind bars.

GIRL MONSTER : THE TRUE STORY OF BROOKEY LEE WEST

SARAH SANCHEZ

One of the most gruesome and bizarre crimes that ever occurred in Las Vegas was discovered on February 5, 2001. The manager of Canyon Gate Mini Storage, Bill Unruh, opened Unit #317 after someone reported a very bad smell.

He found a 45-gallon garbage container that had a brownish liquid oozing out of it at the bottom. He called police.

Detectives entered a unit that contained normal items on one side and the oozing sealed-up garbage container on the other side. There were also books about witchcraft and Satanism in the locker.

Unruh told police that the unit had been rented in the names of Brookey Lee West and Christine Smith on June 26, 1998.

The garbage container had been made airtight with duct tape, packing tape, plastic wrap, and garbage bags. The leakage was coming from a hole that had developed in the bottom.

When investigators cut the container open, more fluid seeped out accompanied by dead maggots. They could see a human body inside, very decomposed. The body was mostly liquefied, but those on scene could easily see that a white plastic bag was tied around the person's face.

Crime scene analysts tested the brownish liquid for human blood and the test was positive.

In the storage unit, Detective David Mesinar found Christine Smith's wallet, ID, prescriptions, and documents relating to her Social Security payments.

Dental records confirmed that the body was Christine's. Christine would have been 68 years old if she was still alive.

Detectives began by looking for Christine's daughter, 46-year-old Brookey Lee West.

Brookey is now serving life without parole for murdering her mother. Brookey may also have murdered her brother Travis and probably murdered her third husband Howard.

Brookey's mother Christine, her father Leroy, her husband Howard, Brookey herself, and Brookey's brother Travis all had tragic childhoods and went on to live destructive or self-destructive lives.

On hearing this story, some might be amazed that nobody killed Christine before she reached her 60s. By all accounts, she was a sociopathic parasite who had never worked a day in her life other than her short degrading stint as a prostitute at the age of sixteen.

By the time her daughter killed her, though, she was a harmless pain in the ass with major health problems and suffering from dementia.

Christine's Childhood

Christine Merle Sands was born on February 14, 1932, in Ennis, Ellis County, Texas. Her parents were Clyde and Annie Sands. As it was for many people during the Great Depression, life was a struggle.

Ennis was a hub for the cotton industry, and Clyde worked as a long haul trucker moving cotton products. He also worked as a lineman installing power lines across the country. The lineman job was very demanding physically, but it paid well when the work was available. Even with both jobs, money was always tight.

Clyde's work often took him away from home for long periods leaving Annie to run the home.

Annie was a housewife and a loving woman. The Sands were not abusive parents, but day-to-day life didn't allow them the time or capacity to nurture their six children.

Trudy was born in 1911. She was followed by Woodrow, Lawrence, Richard Bob, Billy, and finally Christine in 1932.

The two youngest children, Billy and Christine, made it to the eighth grade before they dropped out of school. Their parents had no concept of the importance of education, so this was not an issue in the family.

Christine later told Brookey that a family member had begun molesting her at the age of eight. Billy knows nothing about this, but such a thing would not have been talked about within a family in 1930s Texas.

Billy does say that Christine was a good girl who started to spin out of control around the age of ten.

When she dropped out of school, Christine was thirteen years old. By sixteen, she had gone off the rails. Says Billy, "I think, personally, she was restless at home by herself . . . she was looking for anything that come along so she could grab a hold of it and get out of little old Ennis."

At sixteen, Christine married a young man. This is how Billy describes him: "He was a bad character. I don't know what in the world she ever seen in him, because he was really something . . . It was bad from the word go. Several people said he treated her like a dog."

Christine and her new husband ran off to Houston. According to Billy's wife JoAnn, the husband was very abusive. Very soon, he had turned her out as a Houston whore. Christine felt degraded and she was very angry. She got her daddy to come and take her back to Ennis.

Leroy's Childhood

Leroy was born in Russia. When he was a baby, his family moved to the U.S. and settled in the hills of Tennessee.

His parents' marriage was violent. His father murdered his mother during a domestic dispute. According to West, "He cut her head off with a machete in Tennessee . . . my dad said his father went to prison for about ten years." Leroy was five at the time.

Leroy's older sisters pinned a note to his jacket explaining that he was an orphan and put him on a bus. He ended up alone on a city street corner. The woman who found him gave him to another woman, an alcoholic who was unable to have children. She and her husband thought that being childless made them look bad so they took him in.

His new parents, named Smith, took him to Arkansas and named him Leroy.

Leroy told his own family later that much of his time as a member of the Smith family was spent living in tents and shacks.

At sixteen, determined to get away from that family, he lied about his age and enlisted in the army. His love of guns began in the army. He also liked the military discipline and the structure it imposed.

By then he was already defensive, antisocial, reclusive, filled with anger, and very racist.

West said about her father, "My dad didn't like nothing that wasn't white. That's just the way he was. I used to tell him, 'You know what, Dad? If you tried to join the skinheads, you would be president of them in six months.' He would be like, 'Yeah, I would be.'"

Leroy & Christine

Leroy Smith was stationed at Fort Bliss in El Paso, Texas, when he met Christine Sands in 1947. It's not clear what she was doing in El Paso, 600 miles from Ennis.

She was sixteen, freshly out of her disastrous first marriage. She had blue eyes, long blond hair, and a sexy figure in a tight dress. He was eighteen and looked very fine in his army uniform. They had a lust-hate relationship from the start. They were both infatuated, but his arrogance ticked her off. Her attitude ticked him off but it also made him want her.

They dated on his weekends off. It was casual for him, but she was not going to let this handsome army guy out of her grasp. Soon Christine was "pregnant."

According to Brookey, "My dad said that's why he married her. He told me he wanted to divorce her after he was married to her for about three months. He said, 'I knew I'd been had.'"

Leroy As A Cop – Leroy Gets Into Drugs

Shortly after the marriage, Leroy left the army and was hired as a patrol officer with the El Paso Police Department. El Paso was crawling with drug dealers, drug smugglers, pimps, and prostitutes in the early 1950s. Whatever his motives may have been when he signed up, Leroy soon dove into the muck.

"This is when my father started using drugs, and this is also about the time my mom started using drugs, too," Brookey says.

Leroy told West that he made extra money by shaking down drug dealers. "He'd take dope from some suspect and give it to some snitch to sell it to somebody."

Leroy's drug of preference was speed. He started taking it because he needed energy when he was on night shift, but soon he was popping pills every day. Being a crooked cop in a city full of Mexican-American criminals was right up Leroy's racist alley.

According to Brookey, "It was getting to the point where he was getting really violent. My dad wouldn't back down from anybody, and he had a real bad temper."

At this time, Christine was also doing drugs and beginning to behave strangely. She began to lie all the time and for no reason. One of her favorite lies was that she was Cherokee. Sometimes she was Apache. According to Chloe Smith, Leroy's second wife, this drove Leroy crazy as he thought of Native Americans as "savages."

The couple's life was out of control before they were even twenty years old, before their children were born.

Leroy cheated on Christine constantly. As a cop, he had a lot of access. Leroy later told Chloe Smith that he didn't even try to hide it from Christine because she wasn't interested in sex anyway. He also thought Christine was crazy.

While Leroy was at work, shaking down drug dealers and getting it on with prostitutes, Christine was either in the bars downtown or sitting in the apartment smoking, drinking, and popping pills.

They were fighting constantly and violently by 1951. One time, Christine, in a drunken stupor, crawled into bed, put a gun to Leroy's head, and pulled the trigger. There were no bullets in the gun so she put it under her pillow and went to sleep. Leroy later told Brookey that he had awakened when Christine entered the room and, knowing the gun was empty, pretended to be still asleep.

Brookey Lee West: "Who knows why? But my mother didn't really need a reason to kill anybody. My mother was a very devious person."

Leroy & Christine Pregnant

In 1952, Leroy decided to leave and move on with his life. That's when Christine announced that she was pregnant.

Leroy later told his second wife, "She never got pregnant, she never got pregnant, never got pregnant. Then, when the pressure was on, suddenly it happened."

Eventually it was obvious that she was telling the truth about being pregnant, but Leroy always wondered if Brookey was really his child.

Brookey Is Born

Brookey Lee Smith was born in an El Paso hospital on June 28, 1953. Both parents fell in love with her sweet nature, brown hair, and hazel eyes. As a toddler, she loved her parents and all she cared about was pleasing them.

When Christine took time off from partying, she took Brookey to Aunt Trudy's house or to the park to play. But both of her parents were drug addicts and alcoholics, so Brookey was often left home alone.

Travis Is Born

In 1956, Christine was pregnant again.

West says, "My dad was furious with her . . . 'You just did this to put another rope around my neck!' I heard that for years."

Travis Lee Smith was born August 29, 1956. West recollects, "My brother was a chubby, heavy baby. They put these striped shirts on him, and he looked like a wrestler."

Unlike Brookey, Travis was a problem child from the start. West thinks he may have had ADHD: "He would chew on Sheetrock . . . he was something else. He was like my mother in that he did not have a good disposition. Him and my mother adored each other."

Little Travis was born with a tongue that was too long for his mouth. This made it difficult for him to nurse from a bottle and he had a speech impediment most of his life. People thought he was slow, but he wasn't. They couldn't understand the language he had made up for himself.

Travis was a biter as a tot, and his mother encouraged him to bite people and children. The other kids called him "the snapping turtle."

Brookey & Travis' Early Life

Family snapshots show that the early lives of Brookey and Travis were not total hell. Their smiles in the pictures show that they had some fun times with their parents. But most of the time they were lonely and abandoned.

Brookey made paper dolls and dressed them up as fantasy queens or princesses. She recalls that she only had one birthday party, because her parents were too busy partying to put it together most years. She looked after Travis for days at a time while her parents were out barhopping.

West says, "We had all kinds of medications in our cabinets. Speed, then tranquilizers to calm [them] down." Her mother told her years later that they were both too strung out to be decent parents.

Leroy Is Fired & The Smiths Move To California

In the mid-1950s, Leroy was fired from the police department. He told Brookey and others that it was because he had borrowed money from the police department – which was apparently a normal thing – but didn't return it as per SOP.

Chloe, Leroy's second wife, thinks that it was something worse than that. Leaving the El Paso PD was a sore topic with him when he met her more than twenty years later. Considering his activities as a cop – shaking down drug dealers, getting snitches to sell drugs for him, and using prostitutes as his personal harem – Chloe may well be right.

In 1959, the Smiths headed west. They stayed in cheap motels in New Mexico and Ventura, California, before they chose to settle in Bakersfield, California.

Bakersfield was an oil city full of Texans and Oklahomans who had migrated there during the Depression. It was a honky-tonk town and Leroy and Christine totally belonged.

Leroy found a steady job putting down carpet in houses and was able to rent a home in a low-income neighborhood.

Brookey describes the neighborhood: "Most of them are just like my parents. Alcoholics, drinkers, partiers, sitting out in front of their homes drinking and working on some old wrecked-out car, saying, 'Go in the house there, baby, and get daddy a beer! Go in there and get me my shotgun!' They'd all be out there shouting at each other in the yard with their rifles pointed at each other."

Leroy and Christine partied hard in the Bakersfield bar scene. Brookey, seven, had to look after Travis, four. Sometimes for two to three days at a stretch.

During work hours, Leroy laid carpet while Christine spent all day in bed recovering. She always had aches and pains. But when Leroy came home and wanted to go out, Christine was ready to party.

How Leroy managed to spend his days laying carpet is hard to guess. He popped amphetamines and tranquilizers, and he drank wine all the time. He didn't seem to care about what booze and drugs might be doing to him.

The Smith Family Goes Downhill In Bakersfield

West described the next step in her parents' spiral: "That's about the time when my parents started going to doctors to get more and more pills. They were writing prescriptions for my parents for painkillers, and then my parents would sell them. Sell them to their friends or whoever wanted them . . . that's how they made their money."

She added, "I took care of them and all their problems. If I could hide something for them, I did. If they told me to lie, I lied. Someone would call up and say, 'Can I speak to your dad?' And I'd say, 'Well, he's not here. He went to a doctor.' Meanwhile, my dad was right there smashed out of his mind."

Around this time, Leroy's drunken rages sometimes became so violent that his spankings left bruises on their bottoms in the shape of his hand. According to West. "There were times that he would spank us with a two-by-four. I'd go to school with bruises all over, but no one ever said anything."

The house was full of guns. They were even underneath the beds and the cushions of the couch. Leroy also carried a gun.

He once threatened to kill a man who was driving too fast in their neighborhood.

He told the guy after pulling him out of his car, "You see all these kids around here? If you want to run over somebody's kid, make sure you run over somebody else's, because if you run over one of my kids, I'm going to twist your head off your shoulders and use it as a doorknob."

Christine was a screamer rather than a hitter. Brookey was afraid of both of them and learned to be careful. Brookey and Travis were treated the way their parents had been treated as children. As objects.

The alcohol, drugs, neglect, arguments, and violence damaged both children emotionally.

Added to that stress on the children, their parents kept splitting up and getting back together. There was constant talk of divorce. Christine would disappear for days and then

Leroy would disappear for days. The children couldn't help thinking that everything was their fault.

Leroy & Christine Break Up – Christine Shoots Her Lover & Goes To Prison

In 1961, Leroy left Christine for a waitress named Faye. He moved Brookey and Travis into Faye's house with Faye's six kids.

Meanwhile, Christine hooked up with a married man. He worked as a mason. They had a steamy romance for a few months. He promised her they would have a new life together somewhere.

According to Christine, they had been planning to kill his wife with "sleeping medicine, a lot of sleeping stuff."

Christine told police in a taped admission: "He wanted me to kill her, and I thought, 'You son of a bitch, if I killed her, where would I be with you?' Who would he get to kill me? That's the way I felt about it."

In the early weeks of 1961, the man told Christine he was going back to his wife. She was angry. She told police later, "I said, 'Well, you know, you can take me to the water, you son of a bitch, but ain't going to drown me because I'll kill your ass.'"

On January 24, 1961, Christine asked the man and his wife to meet her at a bar in Bakersfield to help her plan how to get her own marriage back on track. She showed up at 7:30 p.m. as arranged. She had a sawed-off 16-guage shotgun on her lap, hidden by her jacket and sweater.

The couple showed up a few minutes later and sat down. Christine reached under the table, pulled the trigger, and shot him.

The man, aged thirty, was rushed to a hospital with blood pouring out of him. His arm had been shattered, but his life was saved through surgery.

Christine, aged twenty-eight, was taken away in handcuffs. She later told police, "I didn't have the least feeling of sympathy. Hell, no." In fact, she bragged about it for the rest of her life. She also told police at the time that she did not know where Brookey and Travis were living.

Life During Christine's Trial

Leroy's relationship with Faye was falling apart. He took Brookey and Travis back to live in Christine's home while they waited for Christine's day in court.

Brookey found this time very traumatic. She was only eight, and her mother's crime was on the television news. She was very ashamed of her mother.

West remembers going with her father to visit her mother in jail and at the trial: "My dad took a dress down to her, and it was a honky-tonk dress with no back, so her lawyers put a sweater around her because they didn't want her in court in that thing. They wrote in the paper that she was a Lolita."

In March 1961, Christine was sent to the California Institute for Women (CIA) with a sentence of fourteen years for assault with intent to commit murder.

Brookey later said, "My mother talked about that shooting like she was some sort of movie star. The first thing out of her mouth about it was, 'Well, you know, I went to prison because I shot that son of a bitch. He deserved it.'"

Christine In Prison

Christine fit in well with the people in prison. She had always been a manipulative person and knew how to connect with people. She worked it there too. As a kitchen worker, she sneaked extra sweets to certain inmates. Some were outraged when she was moved out of kitchen duty to another job.

Brookey & Travis After Christine Is Sent To Prison

Brookey, aged eight, didn't fare well after all of this. She couldn't pay attention in school. She didn't talk about her situation to friends or teachers. She failed second grade.

Travis, aged five, was completely traumatized. Leroy told Brookey to be an adult and tell Travis that his mother was dead and buried. If she was to be treated as an adult, she should act like one. She did what she was told.

Within a year of Christine being in prison, Leroy and the kids lived in Fresno, then Oregon, then San Luis Obispo, and ended up back in Bakersfield.

As Brookey describes it, they were always worried, they were always moving, there was always trauma. She says of her dad, "Drink all day and half the night. It was getting to where he couldn't even work anymore. We were living in another run-down motel, and he was feeding us crackers for dinner. Pillar to post and motel to motel. If you didn't have something to eat that day, you asked the neighbors for something."

Orphanage

In 1962, Leroy decided that the children would be better off without him. His drinking was more important than looking after them, maybe. They had not heard from their mother since she'd gone to prison.

He dropped them off at the Sunnycrest Home for Youths in Bakersfield. Brookey was screaming that she would be good if he let them come home.

As it turned out, Brookey and Travis loved the orphanage. They went to school regularly, they got good grades, they were properly fed, and they had clothes to wear. The place was run by a loving older couple.

Travis, in particular, became attached to the couple. Brookey did not miss her parents. Both of them would have loved to stay there forever.

Christine Gets Out Of Jail, The Smiths Move To San Jose

One day, Leroy showed up at the orphanage with Christine in the car. She had been paroled after serving only two years of her sentence. She had five years of probation to go yet. Travis cried and screamed – he did not want to leave the orphanage. But leave he did.

Brookey Lee West's take on this is that her parents "sought each other out after my mom got out of prison because it was one of those types of relationships, like when an abused woman keeps going back to her husband. They didn't want each other, but then, when they were apart, they really did. And then, they didn't want each other again. That's the way their relationship was. On and off all the time."

San Jose

In 1965, the family moved to San Jose, now known as Silicone Valley. Any stability the children had enjoyed at the orphanage was gone forever now. Christine was back in their lives and San Jose was where Leroy would dedicate himself to Satan.

Leroy got another job laying carpet and rented a house on Lafayette Street, a mostly Hispanic neighborhood.

Brookey, as a white kid, didn't fit in. She played alone or with her brother.

She says, "The kids weren't very friendly to me. I was always big for my age, and by the time I was twelve, I was tall. I didn't look twelve, and I didn't look like everyone else."

Travis, only nine, was self-destructive and he was fighting. "My brother started using drugs when he was nine," Brookey says. "Pills right out of the cabinet. The bathroom cabinet couldn't hold all these pills. Any color you wanted."

Leroy Embraces Satanism

The family had a friend who lived about six blocks away that West only knows as "Mrs. Beauford." Leroy was especially close to her.

One day, Brookey, aged thirteen, was sent there by her mother to return a borrowed dish. "I knocked on her door, the door sort of came open and I said hello, and nobody answered. I stood there for a second, and I hear this moaning, groaning, kind of like screaming. It's coming from the basement."

When she went to the back of the house, she saw a bunch of people doing a spell or something.

Leroy got into the spells and witchcraft quickly. The idea of making enemies suffer was enticing to him. By the late 1960s he was a regular participant in the ceremonies with all the candles, robes, and chants that anyone might imagine.

Of course, none of this was unusual in California in the 1960s and 1970s. But Leroy started to believe that he was a warlock with a high rank in Satan's legion.

West's take on this: "He had books, knives and other stuff. They wore their robes, almost like the Ku Klux Klan, and it was a secretive organization . . . My dad identified with that stuff. He didn't go around killing people, but he believed Satan was the ruler of this world, and he could give you anything you wanted. You just have to know how to get in touch."

West claims that she understands all of this, has read a lot about it, that it is valid, and that true believers can actually cast spells that work. She says she has not practiced it herself but knows of people in very high positions who do.

Brookey In High School

At the age of fourteen, Brookey was attending Santa Clara High School in Jan Jose. By this time she was very attractive. She had hazel eyes, curly brown hair, a shapely body, and gorgeous legs from doing ballet. She wore the same type of clothes her mom had worn in the Bakersfield honky-tonk days.

West: "I dressed very sexy. I was a looker. The boys all wanted a date with me, but I didn't want to go. I was very standoffish about men. Probably because of the way my home life was, I couldn't invite anybody home."

She had lower than average grades, she was aimless, and she had no plans.

Smith Family Late 1960s

In the late 1960s, Leroy wasn't trying to hide his affairs. He was also drinking very heavily. Christine was fed up and moved out. The resulting divorce was traumatic for Brookey and Travis.

Travis simply dropped out of school to do drugs. It was all he cared about ever again, really. He loved speed and meth. He didn't want to work, though Leroy tried to get him involved in the carpet laying job. He lied and stole to get drugs and was always in legal trouble.

Christine, after years of doing drugs and booze all day every day, joined Alcoholics Anonymous and was eventually successful at quitting both.

She joined a church and got Brookey to attend services with her. She wanted to understand all the traumas of her life, the molestation, being turned into a hooker by her first husband, why she married so young in the first place. Christine wanted to find God. Soon she was able to talk a good game about Jesus but, according to West, she wanted to be forgiven without putting in the work.

Christine was still full of spite and anger.

West explains: "My mom started going to church with me when I was in my teens, but she still viewed religion as a matter of convenience. She wasn't book smart enough to learn the Bible, or even read it, and she didn't apply herself."

Christine Is Actually Crazy

Christine had always experienced aches and pains, she always had a cough, she was always sick in bed. Even with her lifestyle – the smoking, drinking, and drugs – these problems were deemed psychosomatic and she was referred to a mental health clinic.

During her screening, she beat the doctor on the head with the heel of her boot. Authorities ordered her to see a state psychiatrist, Sydney Goldstein. She was a patient of his for the next ten years.

During one visit, Goldstein's receptionist told Brookey that Goldstein only took the sickest of patients. That's when Brookey first understood that Christine was seriously mentally ill.

She had an opportunity to snoop her mother's medical file, and in it she read that her mother was a "sociopath with psychopathic tendencies." Sociopaths care for nobody but themselves.

When discussing this eye-opener, West said, "She was a total sociopath."

Brookey Launches Out On Her Own

Brookey Lee Smith graduated from Santa Clara High School in 1971. It was time to get away from her insane mother, her Satanist warlock racist father, and her dropout druggy brother.

Her grades were lower than average, but she was accepted into the army. The army was not what she had imagined it to be. All the rules and restrictions seemed stupid to her. After nine months, she managed to get out honorably. She had wanted to be a spy.

She was broke and had no post-secondary education. At twenty years old, she was living with Christine, paying all the bills by working odd jobs, waitress jobs, legal secretary jobs. Christine had no job and Brookey desperately wanted to get away from her.

1973 – Brookey Has A Daughter

In 1973, Brookey met a man at the church she and her mother had been attending. Soon they were dating. He was handsome and smooth-talking. She considered him the love of her life.

Ronald Ray Veramontes "was good looking, he was charming, so we dated for a while," says West. "We dated maybe six or seven months, and I was wild about him. I was in love with him. Completely gone."

Veramontes later told police that their relationship had never been serious.

Brookey got pregnant during a weekend trip to Los Angeles. "I just told him I was pregnant, straight up, and it was over the phone, because he called me to see how I was feeling. That's when he gave me this snotty-assed remark, saying, 'How do you know it's mine?' I'm naïve up to this point. I think I knew in my heart he was already out seeing other women on the side, but I really couldn't face that. As soon as I told him I was pregnant, he was gone," she said.

Brookey's parents were furious. "They called me all kinds of names. Bitch, whore, slut, a tramp. 'Why don't you have an abortion?'"

In 1974, at O'Connor Catholic Hospital, Brookey gave birth to a beautiful girl.

1977 – First Marriage Fizzles

Around 1977, Brookey saw a classified ad looking for a female singer for a country band. She was twenty-four and it sounded like a way to make some extra cash. The ad had been placed by a fifty-eight-year-old concert promoter who was an Okie to boot. He was infatuated with her and they were married within a few months.

"He was real good to me at first," she says. "The one thing I always thought was real good about him was he never tried to hit me, never tried to raise his hand toward me, even though we had some nasty arguments. That's the good things I can say about him. But he had drinking issues, dope issues, same thing all my husbands had. I guess it was the caretaker syndrome."

She sang in the band for a while. "You have to be drunk to sing that stuff," she said later.

She wasn't into singing in the band. After about six weeks, she said to him, "Who the hell are you? What do I want with you? This is just not working." They divorced.

1981 – Career In Silicon Valley Takes Off, Second Marriage Fizzles

Brookey eventually got a decent job as a security guard at National Advanced Systems, a computer company located in Palo Alto. Soon she became a secretary there, a much better job, and that is how she met her second husband "West."

She took some papers to his office. He asked her out. They became engaged during their first date and were married within five months. Brookey was twenty-eight and he was forty-nine.

According to Brookey's description, "He was tall, slender, very Norwegian, with sharp features. Good-looking, blond haired."

Christine didn't approve of Brookey marrying a man so much older. Mr. West though Christine was crazy and mean. They couldn't stand each other. They constantly fought. This marriage was also over within months.

Brookey blames her bipolar disorder for both of those marriages. She wasn't stable then, she says. She has a hatred for West that she doesn't have for her first husband.

She says that West molested her daughter during a school vacation. "If I would have had a reason to kill somebody, it would have probably been him. If I wanted to kill him for money, it would have been ideal, because he had $250,000 in life insurance," she says.

Before the divorce, she was set to inherit his estate if he died. "He signed everything over to me in case of his death, so if I had a reason to kill somebody, it would have been him."

Brookey Wants To Give Her Daughter Away

Brookey was working long hours as a legal secretary to support her mother and daughter. When the child was four, Brookey sent her to a boarding school in Arizona so she would not have to be left alone with crazy Christine. There weren't a lot of visits back and forth.

By the time her daughter was nine, around 1983, Brookey decided she wanted her daughter to stay with the people who ran the school. Brookey had mood swings. She was unstable. She did not think she could be a good parent.

But her daughter's father, Ray Veramontes, refused to give up his parental rights. He wanted to adopt her rather than let her be given away.

West was furious with him and so was Leroy. No Mexican was going to tell his daughter what to do.

According to Veramontes, "I wanted to have custody of my daughter, full custody. It was not up for conversation with them. It wasn't in their heads."

Veramontes Receives Witchy Threats

On January 14, 1985, a man dressed in black showed up at Veramontes' grandmother's house asking for "Ray." One witness said the man was wearing a Halloween mask. He shot her in the chest with a .22. With surgery, she survived.

On February 13, Veramontes received a handwritten letter with a pentagram drawn on it and satanic chants threatening the murder of his entire family. "You pray to your God, I'll pray to mine. We'll see whose God is stronger," it said.

He knew that Leroy was a warlock or a witch. Veramontes was terrified of what Leroy might do and gave up his custody battle. His daughter was adopted by the teachers in Arizona.

Brookey's Tech Writing Career

While working at National Advanced Systems, Brookey was promoted from her secretary position to working with hardware and mainframes. She was also studying everything she could find about programming, engineering, and troubleshooting. She was drawn to technical writing and turned out to be extremely good at it.

By the late 1980s and early 1990s, she was doing technical writing on contract for the best companies in Silicon Valley – including Sun, Intel, and Cisco – earning $65-$100 per hour.

She bought a house in Los Banos, wore expensive clothes, and drove a Jaguar.

But she still had Christine around her neck.

Brookey's Life With Christine

Christine was living with Brookey and living off Brookey. They lived together in a rental house in San Jose in the early 1990s before Brookey bought the house in Los Banos. Brookey was kept on her toes just trying to make sure her mother didn't do anything crazy.

Christine tried to poison a neighbor's dog with cayenne pepper and then with gopher poison. When Brookey asked her about it, Christine said, "Yeah, I did. I hate that son of a bitch." The dog survived.

Though they were always fighting, they also loved each other. Brookey had absorbed Christine's obsession with Native American culture. Now they were both claiming Native American roots, and they loved shopping for Indian jewelry and art.

Leroy Post-Christine: Chloe

Leroy's second wife, Chloe, had been through two failed marriages by 1975. She had two children from her first marriage. They were living with their father. She met Leroy while she was working at a tavern near Santa Clara University.

Chloe was born in Massachusetts. Her alcoholic father moved the family to rural Arizona in the 1940s. Their life was "pretty desolate and pretty awful."

Leroy was affectionate and protective. He made her feel special. They were married in 1977 and she hoped this marriage would be different.

They rented a house on Lawrence Street in San Jose. Leroy was still working as a carpet layer. Women still made him "sparkle and twinkle." He was still a hostile person who did not trust people. But he loved Chloe unconditionally and thrived on her stable nature. Chloe was so unlike Christine.

He came with a lot of baggage. He was always falling off the wagon. He was still a raging racist. He had guns hidden all over the house. During arguments, he would threaten to do to Chloe what his father had done to his mother.

During the twenty years they were married, Leroy explored a variety of religions. Chloe never saw Leroy engaged in any kind of devil worship, though in hindsight she can think of a couple of instances.

On one occasion, his Mexican neighbors had been parking in front of his house and he left them a satanic note similar to the one that Veramontes had received. He had an excuse for that – Mexicans are very religious and using religious stuff is a good way to get under their skin.

Another time, after Brookey and Christine had dropped off some furniture and Leroy was putting it in the garage, Chloe saw him sealing a grotesque Halloween mask into a cabinet or a wall. He said it belonged to Brookey and Christine.

She loved him and he was a good husband. He took over all the housework when she went back to school to get a business degree. He was kind and considerate. He wasn't drinking *all* the time.

He had one rule only: Chloe should never associate with Christine because Christine was crazy. She should keep Brookey at a distance too. Chloe would have liked to get together with Leroy's ex-wife and children for holidays, but Leroy explained that they were crazy and not good people.

Whenever Brookey or Travis showed up to discuss something with Leroy, they walked past Chloe, straight into Leroy's office as if Chloe didn't exist.

Only after twenty years of marriage did Chloe see Leroy's frightening side.

Travis Post-Childhood

Chloe did have some contact with Travis. He was not as *persona non grata* as Christine and Brookey were.

Travis was tall and large with long, bushy black hair. He was incapable of holding a job and was often homeless due to his drug addiction.

Chloe: "I don't think he even graduated from the seventh grade. He started using drugs very young, and I think he burned himself out. He did poorly in school, and I just don't think he was very smart. He didn't get it."

Leroy was always trying to help Travis. Brookey could take care of herself but Travis could not. Leroy bought him vehicles, got him flooring jobs, found him apartments. But Travis was too busy partying to take advantage of any of the help.

Leroy started his own flooring business in San Jose – Smith's Floor Covering – so he could hand it over to Travis at some point. Leroy shut it down within a few months and started doing security work.

In the early 1980s, Travis hit bottom. He was in his late twenties or early thirties. He lived on drugs and booze and on the streets. He ate one meal a day at a soup kitchen. He was arrested at least ten times in a period of seven years for public intoxication, loitering, drug related offenses, arson, and attacking an ex-girlfriend during a meth trip.

Brookey West: "My brother liked speed, meth, and he had some guns. He and a friend went over to this gal's house, and they broke in, and she was in bed with this other guy.

So my brother strips them all down naked, and he goes in another room, and he gets this woman's little boy, and he brings him back in, and he says, 'Now you see what a whore your mother is?'"

Someone heard the commotion and called 911. Travis landed in jail.

Brookey continues the story, "By the time he calms down in jail, his hand is broke, his nose is broke, and they were like, what do you expect? So he was going to go to prison for a long time."

He didn't though. Travis was diagnosed as a schizophrenic, judged criminally insane, and sent to Atascadero State Hospital at San Luis Obispo.

Chloe and Leroy visited him there one Christmas. Chloe brought cookies that she had baked for him.

"He came across as a big guy with all this hair," she said, "but to me he just seemed like this big, harmless woolly bear."

Travis cried when Chloe hugged him.

When he was released, Travis went back to the streets. Leroy continued to try to help him get work, but Travis was physically disabled because of his years of doing drugs. At that point, all Leroy could do for him was set up a bank account so Travis could receive his disability checks.

In the early 1990s, Leroy tried one last time to convince Travis to get off the streets and come home. "Dad, I don't want you coming down here anymore," Travis said. "I like living on the street. I've got lots of friends. When you come down here, you just bother me, you disturb me. I don't want you coming down here anymore. I want you to leave me alone."

Christine's Love Life Post-Leroy

In the early 1980s, Christine, now in her early fifties, wanted a man. She came on to workmen and other men, but was always rebuffed. They found her weird. That must have been distressing for someone who had always been so desirable to men.

She honed in on her chiropractor, successful and divorced.

She made a pornographic audio tape of herself masturbating and panting about her love for him. It sounds like a tape intended for someone already involved in a physical relationship with the sender. But the doctor was not remotely interested in Christine.

At one point in the tape, she interrupts the porn for twenty minutes to include a speech from her favorite televangelist who was on TV celebrating the Fourth of July.

According to West, Christine had become obsessed with religious imagery by this time.

After the sermon, Christine's tape goes back to moaning and groaning. She begs the doctor for a secret place for the two of them to be together.

Christine didn't end up giving the tape to the chiropractor because his secretary told her about some other woman the doctor was in love with. The relationship had existed only in Christine's mind, but she was very angry with him.

She told Brookey, "I'm going to get me a gun, and I'm going to shoot that son of a bitch, just like I shot that other one." Brookey refused to get her a gun.

Mother & Daughter Shoplifting Team

Christine and Brookey were caught a few times shoplifting blouses, scarves, and jewelry from high-end department stores. They worked it as a team.

In 1985, Brookey was caught and pleaded guilty to misdemeanor theft and paid a fine. Later that year, when they were arrested after shoplifting together, Christine was upset that the police found Brookey's arrest record but did not find Christine's own conviction record. So she bragged to them about having shot a man.

Mother and daughter were convicted of burglary and conspiracy and sentenced to thirty days in jail and two years of probation.

1993 – Brookey's Third Husband, Howard

In late 1993, Christine and Brookey went to an A.A. meeting at the San Jose Indian Center. Brookey was wearing trampy clothes and Elvira-ish makeup, looking like she wanted to cause trouble. Christine dished out her alcoholic stories and her prison stories and thumped the bible a bit. When the meeting was almost over, Brookey went on a tirade about her ex (West) and how he deserved to be dead.

Everybody at the meeting was afraid of Brookey. Nobody believed the two were Native American.

Later that year, Brookey took up with a man from the Native rehab house next to the Indian Center, Wayne Ike.

Ike said, "She wanted to marry an Indian guy." He loved the sex. But he sensed something was wrong with her. For example, why was this prosperous woman hanging out at a Native rehab center?

Ike also didn't like what she said about kids – she didn't like them and she had given her daughter away. He didn't like how she always talked about money. And he didn't like it when she pulled a gun on him and said, "If I ever catch you messing around, I'll use this on you. If I catch you fucking around, I'll shoot your ass."

Once Ike decided that West was crazy, he hid whenever she came around.

In 1994, Brookey changed her focus to a different man at the halfway house, Howard Simon St. John. She had a good job, a nice car, and a nice house. Howard was a homeless drunk and a drug addict.

Howard's Background

Howard was a child of the South Dakota Sioux, a very noble tribe. He was born on May 15, 1958. He'd had some childhood traumas and been ostracized by his family. He had been drinking regularly since the age of sixteen. His family moved back and forth between South Dakota and California a few times. The last time they left California, Howard dropped out of high school and stayed in California.

He loved partying and he loved booze. He was talented at tweaking cars and often worked for his friend Tony Mercado as a mechanic.

During his mid-twenties, Howard drank until he was unconscious every day. He could down a bottle of tequila. He was also getting into cocaine. He was living on the streets. He already had a huge beer belly and rotten teeth.

By 1988, Howard, aged thirty, was about as low as anybody can go. He'd been arrested for drunk driving, assault and battery, public intoxication, and had been convicted of a felony.

His parole officer wrote that Howard "consumes three to four bottles of hard liquor per week; five cases of beer per week. Drug usage includes peyote during Indian ceremonies only. Cocaine began in 1983. Occasional use. No marks on arms."

Howard's friend Thomas Gutierrez said, "He'd get in fights, he'd get beat up, or he used to get rolled. He would get rolled a lot on the streets. He would pass right out, and people would take his money. He'd be walking downtown, and he would just pass out against a building or something."

In the mid-1980s, Howard found the Native American Indian Center in San Jose and eventually moved in to the halfway house next door. There, Howard lived with eight other end-of-the-line Native alcoholics and started going to Alcoholics Anonymous meetings.

That halfway house is where Howard met Brookey Lee West while Wayne Ike was hiding from her.

Brookey's take on Howard: "When I first met Howard, he looked kind of bad. He was real overweight, and his hair was sort of long. Yet I could see that if he lost some weight and, if he got his hair cut, he would be really good-looking . . . I view life this way – people can be down. They can be sick and they can have a lot of bad things happen, and they can pull themselves back up. That's the way I saw it."

She gave Howard's friends the willies. And they couldn't understand why such a successful woman would want to be with such a loser. They warned him to watch out for an insurance policy.

Howard laughed off his friends' misgivings.

1993 – House In Los Banos, Neighbors On Fir Street, Christine Is Whack

Brookey bought a house on Fir Street in Los Banos in 1993. She brought Christine there to live with her.

Brookey told the neighbors that she had bought the house with a GI loan. She told them that she was a sergeant and that she had flown planes. She also told them the truth, which was that she was a technical writer.

Christine was thin and frail. She had a long braid that hung down to the middle of her back and she always wore a gray sweat suit. Christine made friends with various neighbors. They thought she was lonely and not getting enough nutrition. They found her colorful and interesting but they also thought she was weird and probably insane. Each of them eventually cut themselves off from her.

Christine told the neighbors that she was a strong Cherokee woman who would not take guff from anyone. She talked about being from Ennis and riding the rails with hobos at the age of twelve and pulling a knife on them when they got fresh. She talked about how her granddaughter had been kidnapped from a department store. She gave them bizarre gifts. One was a pair of earrings made out of potatoes.

People who visited Christine saw a room in the house that contained a rack of clothes with the price tags still on them. Some visitors wondered if the reason all those clothes were in the house was because Brookey was running prostitutes. They only had Brookey's say-so that she was a tech writer in Silicon Valley.

Christine would walk into somebody's house unannounced. She and Brookey tried to sell a car to a neighbor for twice what it was worth. Christine brought a neighbor some soup that tasted like pure salt. She claimed she could make love potions.

Christine was proud of her violent history. She bragged about shooting a man in Bakersfield. She said she had been on Death Row until the man came back to life in the morgue. The neighbors knew that was impossible.

Neighbor Laura Parra thought that Brookey looked creepy and might be on drugs.

Everybody could see and hear mother and daughter screaming at each other. They heard Brookey calling her mother a crazy bitch. Brookey told Laura that she didn't like her mother.

Laura: "Brooke said her mom was a lunatic, she was driving her crazy and she didn't want her mom around . . . she talked about what a pain in the ass her mother was, and her exact words were, 'She's a crazy bitch, and I can't wait to get her out.'"

1994 – Brookey Marries Howard

Howard moved into Brookey's new house early in 1994. Whatever good habits had rubbed off on him at the halfway house were gone. He was drinking again. He drove the neighbors around the bend. He stumbled around drunk out of his mind. He was noisy and rude, he slammed doors, he looked ragged, and the neighbors often heard cursing and bottles breaking.

Some tried to interact with him, but Howard was shy and usually wasted.

A few homes on the street were burgled after Howard moved in, and the neighbors wondered if Howard and Brookey were involved.

His father would not let him get married on the reservation in South Dakota, so Howard and Brookey were married in Reno on April 30. Brookey showed Howard's friends a $20,000 ring that Howard had bought for her, but his friends knew that she had to have bought it for herself.

In their collective opinion, Howard was playing with fire.

Christine and Howard could not stand each other and fought constantly. Brookey bought Christine a van, drove her with her possessions to Santa Clara, parked the van in a parking lot, and told Christine not to come back. According to Leroy, that seemed normal in the relationship dynamic between Brookey and Christine.

Back on Fir Street, Sandy Corona started a Neighborhood Watch program. The only people in the neighborhood not invited to the first meeting on May 21, 1994, were Brookey and Howard. The next day, Sandy found a pile of crushed ice in front of her door. Down the street, she saw Howard toasting her with a bottle of Coke. Sandy was terrified of Howard.

There seemed to be more patrol cars around since Howard had moved in. Sometimes the police visited Brookey's house and the neighbors wondered if it had something to do with the clothes that looked stolen. They wonder if Brookey was a drug dealer. And the husband was always loaded.

Howard's friends continued to worry about him. They knew he didn't fit in where he was living. They didn't trust Brookey.

They visited him in the spring of 1994 and they loved the place. They left within an hour. They didn't like being around Brookey.

Burning The Jaguar

A few weeks later, Howard visited his friends. He told them that Brookey wanted him to burn the Jag for insurance money and he asked his friend Thomas Gutierrez to help him. Gutierrez refused, saying that it would be too easy for the cops to get evidence.

On the night of March 3, 1994, an anonymous caller reported a car fire to 911. When the police showed up to the dirt road, they found a burning 1989 Jaguar – a write-off.

Brookey reported her Jaguar missing about fifty minutes later.

She claimed the car had disappeared while she and her boyfriend were at dinner and a movie. The insurance company paid out $18,897. But they were suspicious about the fire and hired a private investigator to look into it.

Days after the Jag burned, Howard showed up in a Corvette to visit his friends. He told them it was a wedding gift from Brookey. Eventually he admitted to Gutierrez that he had burned the Jag. He said he was nervous because the insurance company was sniffing around.

Howard had just married a woman he hardly knew. Now he was committing crimes for her. Gutierrez again expressed his grave concerns that being involved with Brookey was dangerous for Howard.

The neighbors on Fir Street saw Howard tinkering with the Corvette. When they asked where Brookey's Jag was, they were told that it had been stolen, stripped, and burned.

Dwight Bell was the investigator hired by the insurance company. He later gave authorities a laundry list of suspicious circumstances about the Jag: the car was reported missing *after* it was found burning, everything that is worth stealing from a car was intact, none of the normal causes of car fires were involved, and he had found metal distortion indicative of the involvement of a flammable liquid.

By May 1994, Bell was sure the car had been torched for the insurance money, but he couldn't get in touch with Brookey and he didn't have much actual evidence.

Brookey Shoots Howard

On May 21, 1994, the people of Fir Street saw Howard and Brookey looking very cozy. Mike Stoykovich from across the street saw them hugging and kissing in the garage. Laura and Fermin Parra saw them dancing and embracing in the garage.

At some point, Howard went over to ask Fermin why people didn't like him and Brookey. He wondered if it was Christine's fault. Howard was very drunk. Fermin was polite but went back into his house as soon as he could and told his family to keep away from the St. Johns.

Later that day, the people of Fir Street heard a gunshot. Some thought it was a door slamming and some thought it was a firecracker. They heard yelling. Then they saw Howard stumbling out of the garage covered with blood and screaming, "She shot me!" Someone ran into Parra's house and called 911.

The police officer who responded saw that Howard had a bullet wound on his neck. He heard from Brookey, "I did shoot him, but it was an accident." He heard from Howard, "Bitch, you shot me. I'm going to kill you." Brookey said that Howard was coming at her so she took her .32 out of her purse and pointed it at him, and it "just went off." Brookey said that she called 911.

Howard was taken away in an ambulance and Brookey was taken away in handcuffs.

Brookey told police that they were cleaning the garage when Howard became aggressive. She said there had been a series of domestic disputes before this. During this one, he was obsessing that she might be leaving him. He wanted to have sex on the concrete floor of the garage. She did not want to do that. He threw a table at her. She took the gun out of her purse and it accidentally went off.

She didn't give the police a good reason why her .32 was in her purse while her other guns were locked up. She didn't give them a reason why she had her purse in the garage.

According to Howard's statement to police, Brookey said to him, "I'm setting you up." When the police asked him why she would do such a thing, he told them, "She's a crazy bitch."

Brookey was charged with felony assault with a gun and corporal injury to a spouse. The charges were dropped two weeks later on May 25.

Howard had been flown to a hospital in Modesto. He had a big hole in his neck but no artery had been damaged. The doctors decided to leave the .32 bullet in his left shoulder.

Howard phoned the insurance investigators from his hospital room. He admitted to burning the Jaguar and told them that Brookey had given him a Corvette as payment.

Within a week, Howard was released from the hospital. He visited his old friends. He told Mercado and Gutierrez that Brookey had ambushed him in the garage. She told Howard she was going to kill him because the insurance people were getting suspicious. She said she was going to burn the house down.

Back on Fir Street, Leroy showed up in front of Brookey's house. He talked to neighbor Mike Stoykovich about Brookey's troubles and said how disappointed he was that she had married an Indian. He also said a few racist things about Indians.

He told Stoykovich he had no plans to get her out of jail until she calmed down.

A couple of days later Brookey was out on her own recognizance and Leroy dropped her off on Fir Street.

Brookey told her neighbors that she was afraid of Howard, that she was getting a restraining order and a Rottweiler dog, and that the shooting had been in self-defense because Howard was throwing things at her.

Howard Goes Back To Brookey

It seemed that the Howard and Brookey saga was over. He'd reported her to the insurance people and she'd had a restraining order placed against him. But within a few weeks Brookey told him she would sign the cars and house over to him if he came back. He did.

Howard's friends told him he was crazy. They told him she would kill him. He just had nowhere else to go.

The insurance investigator, Bell, eventually found Howard. He was very drunk, sitting on a bench outside a hospital where he was scheduled to have treatment for his neck wound. While Bell talked to him, Howard chugged a couple of airplane bottles of tequila and chased them with Coke.

He told Bell he had already snorted ½ a gram of meth and drunk six or seven airplane bottles of tequila.

Howard told Bell that he made up the whole story about doing the arson to punish Brookey for shooting him. He gave Bell the original alibi about dinner and a movie. He talked about Brookey's work and his own hernia. He claimed that Brookey had to shoot him because he was slapping her around.

Later he admitted to his friend Tyla Knotchapone that if he'd never met Brookey he wouldn't have a bullet in his neck. "I just want to forget her. She is bad news. I think she's going to kill me," Howard told her.

According to Tyla, "He was in tears, actually. He said, 'I can't believe I have this kind of problem in my life with a woman. This woman is dangerous, Tyla. I don't know how to go about divorcing her. It's like she's got me in a web, and I know the way out, but I'm scared. What could be next? I'm scared to find out.'"

Howard described to Tyla how Brookey abused her mother physically and verbally. After offering him a room at her place, Tyla asked him why he'd gone back to Brookey.

"I'm so stupid," he said. "I don't know why."

Brookey Goes Missing

On June 2, 1994, Brookey ran out into the middle of Fir Street shouting that Howard was threatening to kill her because she had misplaced their wedding photo. The police took her to a coffee shop and she told them she was going to divorce him.

Howard, worried about her, spent the next two days looking for her. He filed a missing persons report on June 4. He thought Brookey had been kidnapped. He pestered the police, but they believed she was voluntarily missing. Howard made some frantic drunken calls to Leroy who assured him that he shouldn't worry about her. Leroy disconnected his phone to get some sleep.

That night, Howard told one of his halfway house friends on the phone that he might have to kill her to get even with her.

Howard Is Shot Dead

Sometime in the twenty-four hours following Howard's last phone conversation, he was shot in the back and his body was dumped near the Tule River in Sequoia National Forest, several hours' drive away from Fir Street.

He wasn't murdered there. He was dumped there like garbage.

Howard's body was discovered in the Forest on June 6, sixteen days after Brookey shot him in the neck and three months after he torched the Jag for her. He had been shot in the back with a .38 handgun.

The police report describes him as a former parolee with eight aliases and fifteen misdemeanors, thirty-five years old, 230 lbs.

It was a sad end to a sad life. People had loved Howard Simon St. John and had hoped that he could turn things around. They will continue to miss him.

When police called Howard's father, Sylvester (no longer disowning him) told them that Howard had been in rehab in San Jose for addiction, that he was married to a woman who lived in Los Banos, and that they had a domestic abuse history.

This led investigators to Brookey.

Brookey had been living in a motel after she left Howard. On June 4, she had picked up Christine at her van in Santa Clara and taken her shopping all day. She went to Silicon Valley to work that night – as a contractor she could work whatever hours she wanted – and the door system showed that she had carded her way in.

Christine and Brookey claimed that Howard had found $3,000 in cash in the house and taken off to Reno to party with friends.

They said that when they returned to the house it was a shambles and that it was full of evidence that people other than Howard had been there that night.

Brookey's story about the whole weekend was full of holes, but investigators were never able to find enough hard evidence to bring charges against her.

Howard's lifestyle offered many other possibilities for why he would have been murdered. Christine herself was a suspect for a while. Investigators believe that, if Brookey did it, both of her parents would have helped her cover it up. The case is officially open to this day.

Thus ended Brookey's third short marriage.

Chloe Sees Leroy's Bad Side

Leroy was diagnosed with brain cancer in 1995 and had a stroke in 1996.

In 1995, Chloe discovered that Leroy had forged her name on twenty-five credit card applications and almost $250,000 in cash advances from those had disappeared. She thought Leroy had given it to Brookey, but Brookey insisted that he had gambled it away.

Chloe also suspected that Brookey had been meddling with Leroy's finances so she would get everything when he died. In early 1996, Brookey told Chloe that she and Leroy had given away his gun collection to pay off thousands of dollars he owed to bookies.

In February 1996, Chloe was looking under Leroy's bed for the titles to six vehicles owned by her and Leroy when Brookey tried to zap her with a stun gun and then tried to hit her with it. Leroy jumped out of his bed and screamed at Chloe that she was a trouble-making bitch. Chloe ran to the parking lot with Brookey chasing her and screaming at her. When Chloe called the police, Brookey drove away.

Leroy told the police that Chloe's story was a lie. Chloe believes that Brookey was trying to kill her and that Leroy was in on it. If Chloe died, Leroy would get $250,000 life insurance which would then go to Brookey when Leroy died. Leroy died two months later.

Thus ended Chloe's marriage with the new and improved Leroy.

Brookey's Fourth Marriage Fizzles: George Burnette

George Burnette, another Native American, looked much like Howard St. John though his black hair hung down to his waist. Burnette and West met in November 1996 at a casino in Las Vegas. Their whirlwind passionate romance began when they spent Thanksgiving Day together.

They were married on January 7, 1997 in Las Vegas.

Within a day of arriving at Brookey's Los Banos house, Brookey told George that she had to go back to Las Vegas to be with her sick mother. The next thing he knew was that Brookey and her car were gone.

He drove to Christine's new apartment in Las Vegas and found that she knew nothing of the marriage. Soon the marriage was annulled. Burnette testified to West's instability at her trial.

Christine Gets A Las Vegas Apartment

In 1997, when Christine was sixty-five, Brookey set her up in a low-rent apartment in Las Vegas. The place was called Orange Door. Christine was still into Jesus and still lying about having Native heritage and still bragging about having been on Death Row for shooting a man. Christine had osteoporosis. Alzheimer's was creeping up on her.

But she became close friends with some of her neighbors. One of them, Alice Wilsey, sixty-six, looked after Christine when Brookey was in California.

Another neighbor, Judy Chang, seventy-four, also enjoyed Christine's company.

Brookey visited often and then moved in with her mother in late 1997. Christine's friends could see that the two loved each other but they also saw the two had bitter arguments.

At some point in 1997, Brookey went AWOL from her job at Hybrid Networks. She had checked herself into a psychiatric hospital. After she got out, she confided more and more in a co-worker, Natalie Hanke.

She told Hanke about a big burglary ring she had once been part of, an exaggeration of her shoplifting escapades with Christine. She told her about Howard's murder and said that she could have done it if someone hadn't beaten her to it. She said her father was a powerful warlock. She talked about how much she hated her mother and what a sociopath and psychopath and financial drain she was. She said that she was going to send her mother to live with Travis who was also a sociopath. They would get along well.

Christine Disappears

Christine was quite sick, bedridden most of the time. The last time Wilsey saw Christine, Brookey was giving her pills, supposedly aspirin. Two days later, Brookey told Chang that Christine had gone to live with Travis in San Jose. This was in February 1998.

West said she had told Christine her only other options were being put in a home or West leaving her there and never coming back. She had driven her to San Jose in the middle of the night, she said.

Christine's friends noticed things that made them suspicious about Brookey's story. They saw some of Christine's possessions in the dumpster. They saw her most prized possessions still in the apartment and believed that Christine would definitely have taken them with her.

On November 11, 1998, Wilsey wrote a letter to the police listing six reasons why she thought Christine had met with foul play. She added that she had witnessed Brookey's violence and mental instability. She outright accused West of killing her mother in a rage. She asked the police to look into Christine's bank account and Social Security checks. She added that she herself was afraid of West.

When she brought the letter to the police, they asked her to come back another day but she never did. She knew that she could be wrong about the entire thing.

Brookey continued to talk about her mother as if she was still a pain in the ass for the whole three years after Christine's friends had last seen her until police discovered Christine's body in the garbage bin.

Natalie Hanke distanced herself from Brookey as she saw more of Brookey's weird side. Brookey continued to rage about her mother. Her Las Vegas apartment was full of weird voodoo-ish things that Brookey claimed were her mother's. The one time Hanke was there, she pretended to be sick just to get away.

Hanke had lunch with Brookey one last time in 1999 during a trip to Las Vegas. Brookey then tried to lure her to the storage locker. Hanke now believes that West was planning to kill her and steal her identity.

Brookey Lee's Luck Comes To An End

In 1985, nobody suspected Brookey or Leroy of any involvement in the shooting of Veramontes' grandmother. In 1985, Brookey and Christine got off with fines and probation for shoplifting. In 1994, it couldn't be proved that Brookey had committed insurance fraud, charges of spousal abuse were dropped, and Howard's murder couldn't be pinned on her. In 1996, she wasn't charged with trying to stun gun her stepmother Chloe.

Then on February 8, 2001, Christine's mostly liquefied body was discovered in the garbage can in the storage unit and identified through dental records.

As the storage locker was in West's name, police got a warrant to search her apartment. They found a key for the storage locker. They found duct tape. They found bank statements showing that $30,000 of Social Security checks in Christine's name had been cashed over the years.

Investigators were not able to catch Brookey at home. But a few days into the investigation, Detective Dave Mesinar saw Brookey's plate number on her truck at a 7-11. Then he saw her inside the store.

On February 8, Brookey was arrested, charged with murder, and taken to Clark County Detention Center without making a statement. She had babbled her face off while being interrogated in the Howard St. John cases.

The next day, she was interviewed by a TV news anchor and said that her mother had died of natural causes and she had put her in the trash bin rather than report the death. This made things easier for Mesinar, because he would not have to look for other suspects.

West's involvement was further confirmed when a single print of hers was found on the plastic that sealed the trash can.

The Investigation

Mesinar received information from Daniel Haynes, an investigator in Howard's murder case, and found out that there had been a plastic bag partially on Howard's face when his body was found.

Haynes gave Mesinar a lot of other information about Brookey's life and background. Mesinar concluded that she was certainly capable of killing.

Investigators and the prosecutor Frank Coumou believed Brookey had killed her mother for the money, out of hatred, and because commuting between Las Vegas and San Jose was inconvenient.

Mesinar and his team dug in and interviewed all the people who had known Brookey and Christine. They spent weeks looking for Brookey's brother Travis but, like Haynes before them, they couldn't find him alive or dead. They did find out that around the time Travis was last seen alive Brookey had written to Social Security to have Travis' checks deposited into an account that she had access to.

Mesinar realized that, if Brookey had killed her mother, her husband, and her brother, she was a serial killer. (It has never been proved that West killed St. John and it has never been proved that Travis Lee Smith is dead.)

The medical examiner wasn't able to confirm that Christine was murdered. Her body was too decomposed. But the pathologists were able to prove murder through maggot evidence.

If Christine had been found dead and then put in the bin, as Brookey claimed, the maggots would have been from blowflies. Blowflies find their way to a corpse almost instantly. But the maggots were from coffin flies not blowflies, indicating that Christine's body had been sealed into the bin before blowflies had a chance to find her body.

Investigators thought it was likely that Christine was still alive when she was sealed in the bin. The lack of blowflies certainly proved pre-meditation.

Trial & Conviction

West pleaded not guilty at a preliminary hearing. The trial began on July 6, 2001.

Brookey's defense continued to be that her mother had a lot of medical problems and died of natural causes. Evidence about Christine's medical history was presented at trial. Brookey discovered Christine's body and put her in the bin so she wouldn't have to deal with police. She was still a suspect in Howard's murder and wanted no involvement with them in relation to yet another death.

She didn't deny spending her mother's checks and the prosecution presented evidence that somebody, probably Brookey, had been cashing them.

The prosecution argued that the motives were hatred and money. After reading Brookey's books from the storage locker, Coumou developed a theory involving Satanism that dovetailed with the way Christine's body had been disposed and the plastic bag on her face. But he left that theory out of the trial, worried about future appeals.

The prosecution tore apart the "living with Travis" story because he'd been homeless and then missing for years. If the jury believed that Christine had been living with Travis for some of the past three years, it would shoot down the idea that Brookey had Christine in the storage locker and was cashing her checks the entire time.

Travis had last been seen in 1993. His last known mailing address was the Los Banos house that Brookey and Christine had lived in. His disability checks were cut off in 1999 when administrators couldn't get in touch with him. His driver's license had been expired for ages.

The judge did not allow the prosecution to hint that Travis might be dead, though prosecutors suspected that Brookey had killed him for his checks.

A slew of witnesses, including West's fourth husband and Natalie Hanke, testified about West's personality.

Closing arguments took place on July 18. It took the jury two hours to find Brookey Lee West guilty of first degree murder. The primary reasons for the conviction were the plastic bag around Christine's face and the maggots being the wrong kind of maggots.

Sentence

In September 1994, Judge Mosley sentenced Brookey Lee West to life without parole. He firmly believed that

Christine had been deliberately suffocated with the plastic bag.

"We've heard two possible explanations. One is that it was a shroud . . . in deference to the decedent's status. And, of course, we've heard the other suggestion – that it was, in essence, what killed her by virtue of suffocating.

"I have to tell you, Ms. West, that the latter is more likely in my view. She was overpowered, this item placed around her face, tied tightly, and she was placed into this garbage container, presumably to suffocate her . . ."

Mosely finished with, "While I think everyone would agree putting someone's mother in a garbage can to bury her is bizarre, placing her in there conscious to suffocate her is not only bizarre – it's criminal. You are sentenced to life without the possibility of parole. That's all."

Appeals

Brookey unsuccessfully appealed her conviction in 2003. Her side argued that a natural death due to medical issues had not been disproved. The appeal Justices said that the circumstances "clearly created a reasonable inference of Smith's death by criminal agency."

The Justices also rejected her lawyer's argument that Judge Mosley had erred in admitting photographs of the victim. They opined that gruesome photos have to be allowed if they help with "ascertaining the truth" and these photos helped jurors to see the importance of the plastic bag.

In 2004, Brookey had hopes of a new trial when it was discovered that a man using her brother's name and Social

Security number had been to the Santa Clara Medical Center in San Jose. Investigators weren't able to track this person down. There is a possibility that this person, Travis or not, moved on to Florida. Nobody ever found him.

Finding Travis wouldn't have helped Brookey though. Her trial jury had heard a recording of her saying, "No one knows where he is and no one has seen him in years," which flew in the face of her claim that Christine had been living with him.

In appealing her sentence in 2006, her lawyer argued that she would have been handed a lighter sentence if Veramontes' evidence about being intimidated with Satanic threats had not been presented.

The Supreme Court of Nevada ruled that she was "not sentenced by virtue of some mistreatment that [she] foisted upon Mr. Veramontes." The judge "felt the evidence was overwhelming as to [her] guilt."

Prison

Brookey Lee West is serving her sentence in the Florence McClure Women's Correctional Center near Las Vegas. She is a model prisoner. She leads a Bible study class. She teaches art. She helps raise awareness and money to help Nevada's wild horses.

She denies involvement in any crimes except shoplifting. She does admit that Leroy sent the threatening letter to her daughter's father. She says that in 1999 she was bringing her mother back from Travis to Las Vegas and her mother died in a hotel room on the way.

In 2008 she was sending product to a man who sells murderabilia online. He sold some of her art and some t-shirts that she had worn and signed. He didn't find a buyer for her fingernail clippings at $19.95.

In July 2012 Brookey attempted a prison break. She changed her appearance and tried to walk out while the inmates were heading to breakfast. Staff recognized her standing near a security gate, right next to the main exit/ entrance.

Judge Donald Mosley said in a TV interview: "It was one of the most bizarre trials I've had in my now thirty years on the bench . . . I never saw one iota of remorse . . . I think, all things considered, Brookey West got exactly what she deserved."

BLACK WIDOW JUDY BUENOANO

ERIN CARTER

Judy Buenoano loved men. But she loved killing them more.

In 1971, she murdered her husband James and nine years later she would kill her own son, Michael. In 1983, she would attempt but fail to kill her boyfriend, John Gentry. She is also believed to have been responsible for the death of Bobby Joe Morris (another boyfriend) in 1978. She was never convicted of the Morris crime, however, as by the time the authorities had connected the dots she was sentenced to death for the murder of her first husband.

But the suspicions didn't stop with the Morris death. Buenoano is also suspected of killing a man in 1974 and in 1980, another boyfriend would die under suspicious circumstances.

Buenoano would become the first woman executed in Florida since 1848 and only the third woman executed since capital punishment had been reinstated in 1976.

She would be sent to the electric chair in 1998. Her last words were that she wanted to be remembered as a "good mother."

Instead, she would go down as one of the most sadistic female serial killers in American history.

This is her story.

EARLY LIFE

Judy was born Judias Welty in Quanah, Texas on April 4th, 1943. Her father was a day laborer at a local farm. Judy would talk about her mother being a full-blooded member of the Mesquite Apache tribe but little did she know that a "Mesquite Apache" tribe didn't exist.

Her mother would die of tuberculosis when Judy was only two years old. She and her baby brother Robert would be sent to live with their grandparents while their two older siblings would be put up for adoption.

"When Judy's mother died," forensic psychologist Paula Orange said. "It sent Judy's life into a tailspin. This is one of those 'Butterfly Effect' scenarios. A tragic circumstance that occurred early in a child's life that led to her perpetuating pain on everyone else for the rest of her own adult life."

She would eventually leave her grandparents and join her father in Roswell, New Mexico. He had remarried and Judy would claim that both he and her new stepmother would beat, starve, and burn her with cigarettes.

They made her a "house slave", forcing her to do chores around the house at their bidding. Judy would finally act out at the age of fourteen as she would burn two of her step brothers with hot grease. Not stopping there, she attacked both her father and step-mom with fists flying.

Police would be called and Judy would be jailed for over two months. After she served her jail time, the judge gave Judy a choice, either return home or go to reform school. She opted for the latter and was sent to Foothills High School. She would remain there until 1959 when she would graduate at the age of sixteen.

She held her entire family in contempt, particularly her younger brother Robert.

"I wouldn't spit down his throat if his guts were on fire," Judy once said when asked about her brother.

CHANGING IDENTITY

Judy returned to Roswell but changed her name to "Anna Schultz". She found work as a nurse aide and would give birth to a baby boy out of wedlock, Michael Schultz on March 30, 1961. Judy would remain silent on the identity of the baby's father but people believed that Judy was having an affair with a pilot from the nearby air force base.

In 1963, the twenty-two-year-old Judy would marry James Goodyear. Goodyear was twenty-nine years old and serving as a sergeant in the United States Air Force.

They would have their first child together, James Jr, four years later. James would celebrate the event by legally adopting Michael. Daughter Kimberly would come a year later as the family would move to Orlando, Florida.

Judy would then open her own business, starting the Conway Acres Child Care Center in Orlando. She listed James as the co-owner even though he was during a one-year tour in the Vietnam War. After returning home, he only had three months of downtime before he was admitted to the U.S. Naval Hospital in Orlando, complaining from symptoms staff physicians never quite identified. He would die on September 15, 1971.

Goodyear was only thirty-seven years old at the time of death and authorities believed he died due to natural causes.

"He came home from Vietnam ill and he never got well," Judy said. ``It had nothing to do with me. I was not in Vietnam."

"Crazy that Goodyear was able to survive the horrors of Vietnam but not Judy Buenoano," Orange said. "He had no idea he was married to a sociopath. She had no respect for the fact that he had just put himself on the line for her and the country. All she saw were dollar signs."

Judy poisoned James with arsenic and waited almost a week after his death before cashing in his three life insurance policies. A few months later, an "accidental fire" burned down their Orlando home. Judy would receive another $90,000 in fire insurance.

She lost her husband and her home. But her purse was never fatter.

NO GRIEVING WIDOWS ALLOWED

Judy would waste no time finding another man. Despite having three kids in tow, she would find a new love in Bobby Joe Morris when she moved her family to Pensacola.

It was business as usual for Judy as she had a fat bank account courtesy of James Goodyear and a new beau in Bobby Joe. Eldest son Michael, however, was not doing well in school. He scored on the low end on IQ tests and was a behavioral problem. Judy would get him evaluated at a state hospital in 1974 and then sent Michael out to foster care where he would also receive psychiatric treatment.

Judy's new home would suffer another "accidental fire" and she collected money from the insurance. She then took Michael out of foster care and moved to Trinidad, Colorado with Bobby Joe and the rest of her children. Judy then changed her name from "Anna Schultz" to "Judias Morris".

FOUR YEARS MAX

Judy would date Bobby Joe for four years before deciding it was time to cut him loose.

Bobby Joe would start to suffer from the same mysterious illness as James Goodyear did years earlier as he complained of dizziness and vomiting. He would be admitted to San Rafael Hospital on January 4, 1978, but doctors would not be able to pinpoint what was wrong with him. He would be sent home to Judy's care two weeks later. Two days later, however, he would would pitch face-first into his dinner plate, unconscious. He would be rushed to the hospital, but Judy knew that her "medicine" had taken effect.

Five days later, Bobby Joe Morris would be dead. Doctors would chalk up his death to cardiac arrest and metabolic acidosis.

Judy would wait, just like she did after she killed James, before cashing in on Bobby Joe's life insurance.

Authorities were none the wiser.

But Bobby Joe's family suspected something fishy was going on. Back in 1974, Judy and Bobby Joe had been visiting Brewton, Alabama when a man from Florida was found dead in a motel room in that town. Police would find the man in the room after receiving an anonymous call. He was shot in the chest with a .22-caliber weapon and his throat was cut open.

Judy's connection to the crime? Bobby Joe's mother had overheard Judy telling her son about the murder.

"The sonofabitch shouldn't have come up here in the first place," Judy said. "If he came up here he was gonna die."

Bobby Joe had told his mother about the crime on his deathbed. She thought the confession could be attributed to his delirium, but Bobby Joe told her too many specifics to ignore.

"We should never had done that terrible thing," Bobby Joe mumbled to his mother. "Never should have done that to him."

She tipped off police but they would not be able to find any fingerprints inside the room and no bullet was recovered from the corpse. The case remained unsolved.

WHAT'S ONE MORE SURNAME?

On May 3rd, 1978, Judy would change her name again. This go around, she would change her last name to Buenoano, which in Spanish meant "good year." She stated that she meant it as a tribute to her husband James Goodyear and her Apache mother.

Things continued to go bad with Michael as he dropped out of high school in the tenth grade. With limited employment opportunities, he would join the army in June of 1979 and get assigned to Ft. Benning in Georgia after basic training. When he was on his way to his new post, he visited Judy in Pensacola.

Judy greeted her son with open arms. Then she began poisoning him.

By the time he reached Ft. Benning, he felt sick. Army physicians would find seven times the normal level of arsenic in his body.

They could do little to reverse the damage done. Six weeks after his arrival, the muscles in his arms and legs and deteriorated to the point where he was a paraplegic.

"Michael had no use of his legs," Orange said. "And he could not move his arms past his elbow. Again, Judy was a sociopath. It is unfathomable for a normal human being, a mother, to do this to her own child. Yet she did it to Michael. He was always an inconvenience to her but now that he had military insurance he could become an asset in death."

Judy would give Michael the short shrift while favoring James and Kimberly. Michael and James didn't get along well as clearly their mother favored the latter. Judy would hide Michael when people came over because she was ashamed of him. She would have a neighbor named Constance Lang watch over him when visitors arrived.

"Michael didn't fit the picture Judy wanted to present to the world," Orange said. "She wanted to be looked at like a woman of high status. She drove a Corvette and owned her own business. Michael was a slow-thinking kid. She didn't want anyone to see that."

The army didn't investigate the reasons behind Michael's inordinate levels of arsenic. Instead, they set him up with leg braces and a prosthetic device on one of his arms.

He would be discharged from active duty because of the medical disability.

But his mother saw dollar signs.

The day after his return home, Judy wasted no time. She organized a fishing trip with Michael, James, and daughter Kimberly. They would leave Kimberly ashore at the East River bridge while they went into the water with a two-seat canoe. A small folding lawn chair had been placed in the middle of the canoe for Michael who had was outfitted with a leg brace, a fishing reel, and a ski belt.

James would state that had fished for about two hours when they were reaching shore when a "snake fell into the canoe." He said that everyone panicked as the snake slithered around. The canoe hit a log and capsized.

James would claim to have been knocked out by the impact and would remember nothing until he came to inside an ambulance.

He would tell this version to the court but when he was talking to Army investigators, he made no mention of a snake.

"There is conjecture as to how much James was involved or much did he know," Orange said. "The statement given to the army investigators is different from what he would state later in court. The statement given to the army was a written statement and the handwriting didn't seem to match his own."

A man named Ricky Hicks saw the overturned canoe, an ice chest, and a plastic bag in the river. He also saw Judy and James.

"I lost the other boy," Judy said as Ricky approached them on the shore. "A snake had gotten into the canoe and I tried to hold the snake down with a paddle."

"Where is he?"

"It's no use," Judy said, waving him off.

Hicks said Judy appeared to be concerned about James then asked him for a beer. He then drove Judy's car to a nearby phone and called the county rescue squad.

The rescue team arrived and began looking for the missing Michael.

The canoe had not moved as there was barely a current. They would find Michael's body one-quarter of a mile upriver where the canoe had been rescued. The rescuers stated that it should not have been a problem to swim upstream, suggesting that Michael could have been saved.

Judy initially said that Michael had a life jacket on but later recanted and said that it was a ski belt.

There was no ski belt on Michael when he was found.

Judy would later state that after the canoe capsized, she saw James lying face down in the water. She swam over and cleared his air passage to resuscitate him. She looked around for Michael then was picked up by Ricky Hicks.

"Michael disappeared under water," Judy said. "I went to rescue James. I almost lost both of my sons that day. Mothers just don't murder their children. If I'd have lost both of them, I don't know what I would have done. They would have had to put me in a mental institution."

"Kimberly's boyfriend would later testify that Judy had killed Michael for the insurance money," Orange said. "The children knew about their mother but she had clearly brainwashed them into silence. She provided for them, she fed them. She knew what was best."

Telling the police that she was a "clinical physician", they bought her story of the boat capsizing. The army investigators did not buy her account. Not having any evidence, however, they would eventually pay her Michael's military life insurance ($20,000). Investigators got suspicious, however, when they found out that two civilian life policies were taken out on Michael. The applications on both policies look to have been forged.

Judy's former sister-in-law, Peggy Goeller, would call to inquire how she was doing. She would make no mention of Michael's death during her first call but on a second call she told Peggy that Michael had died "during Army maneuvers".

MOVING ON

Judy would demonstrate very little grief over Michael's death and she would not be charged with his murder. Foremost on her mind was finding another man and another big check.

She opened a beauty salon in Gulf Breeze and found her next mark: businessman John Gentry.

Gentry was more well-heeled than her previous conquests so Judy put on airs for his sake. She told him that she had Ph.D.'s in biochemistry and psychology and was the former head of nursing at West Florida Hospital.

Gentry believed her story and decided to spoil his blue-blooded girlfriend expensive gifts, vacations and the finest cuisine all in the name of courtship.

Pushing the envelope, Judy would encourage John to provide life insurance for both them both. She then secretly boosted Gentry's coverage from $50,000 to $500,000 without him knowing.

Two months later, Judy began giving Gentry "vitamin pills".

"Come on," she said, placing two pills into Gentry's palm.

"What are you, my mother?" Gentry asked.

"Well, God forbid I want to see you healthy," Judy slid the cup of water toward her prey.

Gentry would then complain of dizziness and later begin vomiting after his daily dose of Judy's "vitamins."

He would admit himself into the hospital and noticed that his symptoms disappeared when he stopped taking the vitamins.

Still smitten by Judy, he did not suspect her of wrongdoing. Instead, he took her vitamins and hid them in his briefcase.

One night, however, Judy sat him down for a special dinner. She had a very special announcement.

"I'm pregnant," she said, smiling in triumph.

"Finally," Gentry said. He told Judy that they should celebrate. She told him to go to the liquor store for an expensive bottle of champagne.

"Be right back," he said, kissing her with excitement.

Running out the door, Gentry got into his car and a bomb exploded with he turned the ignition key.

Amazingly, Gentry survived the blast as trauma surgeons saved his life.

"Judy really overplayed her hand with the explosion in the car," Orange said. "Really it speaks to her level of dedication and ingenuity. Who knows where she got the idea, maybe watching the Godfather. But the police found the dynamite residue inside Gentry's car. They decided to look no further than to Judy herself."

Their interrogation and research would unearth lie after lie. They found out about the $450,000 increase in Gentry's life insurance.

Gentry himself thought the insurance had been canceled. He was shocked to learn that she had increased the payout and was paying his premiums out of her own pocket. The police didn't spare him any quarter. They would him that she was not a real doctor and that she couldn't get pregnant.

"What?" Gentry muttered, completely flabbergasted.

Judy had been sterilized seven years earlier.

Gentry couldn't believe his ears. Police would go on to say that she had booked tickets for a world cruise for herself and her children...leaving Gentry out. They discovered that Judy had been telling her friends that Gentry was suffering from a "terminal illness."

The only "terminal illness" Gentry had was Judy Buenoano.

Now fully convinced, Gentry would reach into his briefcase and give police the "vitamin pills" that Judy had been giving him.

"Judy was emptying the vitamin casing and filling it with formaldehyde and a little arsenic," Orange said. "Over time, this would have been lethal."

The state attorney would refuse to charge Judy as they wanted an air tight case in order to prosecute. Knowing that they had their killer, officers, and federal agents searched Judy's home in Gulf Breeze, obtaining wire and tape from her bedroom that looked to match the same wire/tape they found on the bomb in Gentry's car.

They would search her son James' room, finding marijuana and a sawed-off shotgun. He would be jailed him for possession of drugs and an illegal weapon.

"Again, this is a strange mistake on Judy's part," Orange said. "She was meticulous and a good liar. Why she didn't remove any and all evidence from her home is a head-scratcher. She had gotten sloppy because she had gotten away with so many crimes before without so much as a slap on the wrist. She thought she was above the law, got careless and left incriminating evidence behind."

Judy would then be arrested at her beauty salon and charged with attempted murder. It took a month of police work, but authorities would trace the source of the dynamite used in the bomb, linking the Alabama buyer to Judy via phone records which showed numerous long-distance calls from her home.

Judy would pay bail but authorities would not let up. Five months later, she would be indicted for first-degree murder in the death of her son Michael, with an additional count of grand theft for the insurance scam.

Feeling the noose around her neck, Judy would fake a seizure and wind up in Santa Rosa Hospital.

Authorities then exhumed the bodies of the men they believed she killed. Bobby Joe Morris was exhumed with arsenic found in his remains. Identical results were obtained with the exhumation of James Goodyear, in the following month.

Connecting the dots, police obtained a court order to exhume the bodies of all the men that had died while associated with Judy; son Michael, husband James Goodyear, and boyfriend Bobby Joe Morris.

Arsenic would be found in all of the bodies.

"There was enough arsenic in him (Goodyear) to kill twelve people," Detective Ted Chamberlain said. "So he was loaded. I mean that boy was loaded with it when he went down."

OPEN AND SHUT CASE

In 1984, Judy would be convicted of the murders of Michael and attempted murder of Gentry. In a separate trial in 1985, she would be convicted of the murder of James Goodyear in which she would ultimately receive the death sentence.

Judy would be imprisoned in the Florida Department of Corrections Broward Correctional Institution death row for women.

HER FINAL HOURS

Judy would spend her last day watching a hunting and fishing show, eating chocolates, and talking about old times with her children and cousin Jeanne Eaton. She would read a suspense novel called "Remember Me" and her last meal with be steamed broccoli, asparagus, strawberries and hot tea.

Judy's impending execution did not receive the same media attention as Karla Faye Tucker whose was executed only a month earlier. Her execution was opposed by the Pope and Jesse Jackson.

'"She may not have been as photogenic, as young or as pretty as Karla, but she was just as good a Christian," Eaton said.

"Judy obviously had her enablers within her family," Orange said. "How could she be 'just as good a Christian' if she is poisoning people, blowing them up and the 'Christian' she is being compared to is ice-picking people to death. People say the strangest things."

But Judy herself was bitter that no one paid much attention to her presence on death row, particularly the fact that she was a woman.

``Karla was a young female, very attractive and she had become a Christian in prison," Judy said. ``We all prayed that she would be granted a stay of execution and clemency because we felt that she was a different person and she deserved a chance. Possibly, I am a different person. But I was a Christian when I came here. I was a devout Catholic. I've not changed in that."

"It was a bit of a curiosity as to why the media was so charged to prevent the execution of Karla Faye Tucker and paid little heed to Buenoano," Orange said. "Tucker's killings were ferocious and sadistic while Buenoano's killings could be seen as passive. But what drew people to Tucker was her physical appearance and demeanor. She came across as a sweet, reformed choir girl at the end. She had a charming smile and a soft voice. Buenoano, on the other hand, looked sinister. She had squinty eyes, high cheekbones and a snarling, Southern drawl. Her body language and demeanor screamed hostile."

Judy would enter the death chamber with several guards by her side. They strapped her into the large oak chair, placing leather straps over her waist, wrists, chest, and legs.

They fitted the calf and headpiece electrodes last, inserting a wet sponge in between to reduce the burning of Judy's skin.

"Do you have a final statement?" the warden asked.

"No, sir," Judy closed her eyes tight.

The witnesses on the other side of the glass partition watched in silence.

Judy did not look at them as a leather mask was placed over her face.

The warden nodded his head and the switch was pulled.

Steam wafted up from her right leg as her body jolted for thirty-eight seconds. Her hands balled into fists, white knuckling from the shock as smoke rose from her feet to the ceiling.

Then Judy went limp. She would be pronounced dead at 7:08 a.m., March 30th, 1998.

The date was her son Michael's 37th birthday.

BLACK WIDOW KRISTIN ROSSUM

AIMEE BAXTER

Photos of a beautiful, lively little girl, her blonde hair in pigtails as she dances The Nutcracker in her little pink tutu. That same adorable child laughingly enjoying holidays with her family at their home. These are the pictures that Constance Rossum will show you of her daughter Kristin.

Bright, vivacious, and uncommonly beautiful are the words used to describe Kristin Rossum as a child. The child that everyone said was so smart and pretty, the one who modeled for department stores and who excelled in her schoolwork, the one with what seemed to be the perfect suburban childhood.

However, as many already know ... looks can be deceiving.

Idyllic Child becomes a Rebellious Teen

Born to Ralph and Constance Rossum on October 25, 1976, in Claremont, California, Kristin Rossum wanted for nothing. Kristin was the first child of Ralph Rossum – a professor at Claremont McKenna College – and his wife Constance – who worked at Azusa Pacific University. Even when her first and then second little brother was born, Kristin remained her parent's sweet little princess.

When Ralph accepted a position as President of Hampden-Sydney College in southern Virginia, the family moved across the country from California to Virginia. It was 1991 and Kristin was a delicate 15 years old. Her parents enrolled her in an all-girl boarding school in Richmond, Virginia named St. Catherine's School.

That seems to be the beginning of the end of Kristin's innocence. At the private school, Kristin made friends quickly and soon was very popular. She became the party girl smoking, drinking, and using marijuana liberally.

In 1992, at just 16 years old, Kristin is introduced to methamphetamines – a strong Central Nervous System (CNS) stimulant – and is soon hooked. Within a few weeks, she was using Crystal Meth (also known as Crank, Speed, Chalk, etc.) daily. She was a tweaker (slang used to describe a methamphetamine addict).

Kristin the Druggie

When asked about it later, Kristin recalled her first time using meth by saying "I remember it feeling good, a kind of euphoria. You feel very revved up and energetic and happy. I wanted to feel that all the time."

Soon, Kristin's straight As were slipping to become Cs and Ds. She lost weight rapidly and began to withdraw from her family and any friends who were not using meth. According to later court records, Kristin is described as having "an almost insatiable need for crystal meth."

It was not long before Kristin developed all the character traits that addicts hone to conceal and continue their freedom to use. Lying, manipulation, and theft became the new norm for young Kristin Rossum.

Her parents were understandably at a loss for how to deal with this behavior. After all, not that long ago they were tucking her into her pink canopy bed and kissing her goodnight with a song and a prayer. However, the lack of consequences established by her parents could be a contributing factor in her later misdeeds.

At first, they ignored their daughter's erratic and rapidly devolving character, chalking it up to teenage angst. Eventually, they could not turn a blind eye anymore and they soon realized that their daughter was not who they thought she was.

Later, both Ralph and Constance cite an incident in 1993 as the first time they admitted their daughter had a problem. After returning from a cruise in April of that year, the Rossums found that their sweet, perfect daughter had in fact stolen their credit cards, personal checks, and a video camera.

Confronted with the missing items, Kristin pointed to some of her friends (fellow druggies) as the thieves. They say that she admitted to using some of the cash to buy drugs but insisted that the rest was stolen by somebody else. Her parents accepted Kristin's excuse and did not report the theft to police.

According to Constance's testimony later, Kristin's erratic behavior came to a head in December of 1993. Ralph Rossum – convinced Kristin was still using drugs – attempted to search his daughter's backpack. She resisted, they struggled, and he struck her several times in the arm to get the bag away from her.

However, that was not the end of the incident. Sobbing and enraged, Kristin grabbed a knife from the kitchen and slashed at her wrists. When that did not work, she ran upstairs to the bathroom, locked herself inside, and began hacking at her wrists with a razor. Later Kristin told the court, "I felt devastated ... I didn't know how to deal with the situation ... I wanted them to see how sorry I was."

Her wounds, however, were superficial and her parents treated them at home. They later said that they were "afraid of what would happen if they took her to the hospital." They feared that if they told the hospital that she had cut herself, they would have committed her for a psychiatric evaluation and if they tested her blood and found drugs, they would report her to the police.

It is likely that the reason none of the cuts were serious was that Kristin did not intend them to be. Psychologists later speculated that it was merely a way for her to manipulate her parents. If it was, it worked.

Again, Kristin escaped any immediate consequences for her bad behavior. Again, her parents made excuses for her behavior and thus enable her to continue that behavior. Cryptically, one entry in her diary after this incident contained the morbidly, prophetic words, "I could get away with murder."

A few days after this incident, a teacher noticed the marks on Kristin (or she possibly showed them to her intentionally). She called the police to the school to investigate the possibility of child abuse.

Officer Larry Horowitz of the Claremont Police investigated and testified that Kristin told him that her father had hit her and that her mother had "called her a slut and said she was worthless." After interviewing Ralph and Constance Rossum, Officer Horowitz concluded that there had been no abuse and the case was closed.

In January 1994, Constance found a glass pipe hidden in Kristin's underwear drawer. She eventually called Officer Horowitz and Kristin was handcuffed, arrested, and held for several hours at Claremont Municipal Jail.

Kristin finally had her first taste of culpability. She seemed to clean her act up and after graduating, she enrolled part-time at the University of Redlands in California. However, soon she relapsed and dropped out of school without a word to her family and simply disappeared. She moved to Chula Vista – a suburb of San Diego near the Mexican border.

A Chance Encounter

After a month of hard partying, drinking, smoking meth, and hiding from her parents, Kristin was walking the pedestrian bridge that led from Chula Vista to Tijuana, Mexico. Authorities speculate that at the time she was likely on her way to meet her supplier in Mexico on that fateful day.

As she crossed the bridge, Kristin Rossum dropped her jacket. Before she could retrieve it, a handsome young man that she later described as reminding her of John Stamos, had picked it up and was handing it to her. It was Greg de Villers and he later told friends "it was love at first sight." They chatted in French while Greg's younger brother paced nearby.

She returned to the Southern California apartment where de Villers lived with his brothers, Bertrand and Jerome, and a friend, Christopher Wren. She never left.

Within a few weeks, the couple was professing their love and de Villers had sworn to help Kristin kick her meth addiction. Greg's brothers and Wren were not happy and prompted him to end the relationship. They had noticed that things were coming up missing from the apartment since Kristin's arrival and knew of her drug problem.

According to a statement given later by de Villers' friend and roommate Christopher Wren, Kristin had told him that she felt like being with Greg was the wrong choice. For some reason, Wren chose not to tell his buddy.

Even if Wren had told de Villers about Kristin's doubts, it is unlikely that it would have made any difference. Greg de Villers was adamant, he loved Kristin Rossum no matter what her faults and he was going to save her from herself.

By May of 1995, it looked as though he had done just that. By all accounts, it looked like Kristin was clean and free of the hold meth had on her. She reestablished contact with her worried parents and it looked like Kristin was finally moving towards the bright future her parents had envisioned for their little girl.

The Rossums looked at Greg de Villers as if he was an angel for all that he had done for Kristin. Constance Rossum, in an interview with the CBS news magazine "48 Hours," put it like this, "We always called Greg our godsend from heaven. I mean, of all the people she could have met, to have met a nice, decent person who wanted to take care of her, we thanked God."

Soon, Kristin enrolled at San Diego State University. Her professors later said described Rossum as a stellar student with one going so far as to describe her as "among the most promising students" he had "ever taught."

Everyone who knew her believed she was happy. She was earning straight As and in 1998, she graduated cum laude (with honors). She got a job at San Diego Medical Examiner's office as a toxicologist.

Constance would later testify, "Our old Kristin was back," and she thanked God and de Villers – in that order – for the change.

Storybook Love?

Everyone who knew them described Kristin and Greg as the perfect couple. Constance Rossum testified later that when they were together they were "like a couple of lovebirds." When they announced their engagement, nobody was surprised.

However, as is often the case, outward appearances did not accurately represent reality. There was a layer of tension beneath the surface of de Villers and Rossum's storybook love affair. Kristin's closest friends knew that she had a hard time staying faithful and monogamous.

According to prosecutor's later, Kristin actually maintained a "graphically flirtatious" correspondence with a former boyfriend and at least one other man during at least some portion of her relationship with de Villers. Rossum even went to her mother only a month before she was supposed to walk down the aisle and broke down in tears as she told her mother that she wanted to cancel the wedding.

Constance Rossum considered her daughter's outburst to be cold feet, pre-wedding jitters that would pass. After all, Greg de Villers was the man who led her out of the darkness of addiction and Constance could not see how Kristin could possibly want to end the relationship.

She would soon tell the court, "I gave her the wrong counsel, I'm afraid."

The wedding was spectacular. The video shows a smiling and laughing Kristin Rossum, now Kristin de Villers, dancing with her new husband and looking happy. As for de Villers, he is recorded on that video saying, "Kristin is the most wonderful person I've ever met. I just can't wait to spend the rest of my life with her."

Only seven months after the wedding, however, Kristin Rossum told her mother that she felt "trapped like a bird in a cage." It was January 2000 and Kristin's journal shows that she had begun souring on her marriage only a couple of months after the wedding.

Greg de Villers did not show any sign that he felt the same or even knew of his wife's misgivings and doubt. Conversely, his brother

Jerome later testified that Greg was ecstatically happy and never spoke of anything even smacking of marital discord. Even his colleagues at a genetics research firm where de Villers worked, described him as happily married and devoted to his wife. Some even went so far as to describe Greg de Villers as "sickeningly in love with his wife."

Friends of Greg de Villers said that he was often talking about his plans for their future together. He bragged about his wife's accomplishments, both big and small, and often spoke of starting a family. One friend remembers him saying that he wanted "all girls who were as beautiful and smart as Kristin."

At the same time, his adored wife was painting a much grimmer portrait of her marriage and her husband. She often complained to colleagues and friends about Greg, saying that he was moody, controlling, and domineering. Later, in an interview with "48 Hours," Kristin said, "Greg became very, very clinging... I tried to pull away and have some sort of independence."

An email sent to her brother Brent only 11 months after the wedding showed how she truly felt. She wrote, "I should have trusted my own instincts and called off the wedding. Now I'm stuck with the heavy realization that I married the wrong person."

A New Love Affair

Not long after Kristin Rossum sent that email to her brother, she met Dr. Michael Robertson. Newly hired as Chief Toxicologist at the San Diego Medical Examiner's office, Robertson was Kristin's immediate supervisor and she began spending large amounts of time with him.

Soon, they were spending time together outside of work. Kristin found danger and excitement in her passionate affair with her handsome, Australian doctor – who was also married. Her husband – and the problems she seemed to have with him – disappeared from Kristin's consideration and soon she was talking with friends outside of her colleagues about the wonderful new man in her life who she described as "a big hunk of an Australian guy."

By early May, Rossum was receiving inappropriate emails and notes from her boss. A search of her desk later turned up love notes and IOUs for things such as "a night of lovemaking" from Robertson. Coworkers later reported that Robertson was often seen sauntering into work with a bouquet of flowers that would soon end up on Rossum's desk.

In June, according to court records, Kristin Rossum had given her lover a gift. A book titled "52 Invitations To Great Sex" she had inscribed on the inside cover, "Well, sweetheart, together we'll enjoy a lifetime of passion."

When asked later, Rossum said, "I felt like I was in love. It was very romantic, very exciting, very passionate."

In August of 2000, Kristin turned to her best friend, Melissa Prager. Prager later told the court that he friend confided in her that she was madly in love with Robertson but was "terrified" by the idea of telling Greg she wanted a divorce.

In October 2000, Greg de Villers was still telling his friends, family, co-workers, and anyone else who would listen about his love for his wife and his plans for their future. His brother Jerome later told the court that around Halloween, Greg was talking about his excitement over taking his future children with Kristin out to trick or treat.

However, Kristin Rossum had reached a conclusion about her marriage. She told her close friends that she was looking for an apartment and planned to leave her husband.

'Til Death Do Us Part

It is unclear how de Villers learned of his wife's infidelity and plan to leave him. Rossum has always claimed that she told Greg de Villers about the affair and that her admission launched a spiraling depression in her husband.

According to Kristin Rossum, she told her husband about Robertson and he demanded the man's phone number. When Kristin supplied the number (although why she would is uncertain), de Villers called her boss and lover and demanded that he break off their relationship.

There is no court record of a response to this demand by Robertson. However, the relationship continued.

Authorities, however, have a very different set of circumstances in mind for how Greg discovered Kristin's infidelity.

They maintain that de Villers found out about the affair on accident in the fall of 2000. This was after Kristin and Robertson were sent to Milwaukee together to attend a toxicology conference. According to court records, despite being booked into separate hotels – likely due to rumors in the office about their relationship – the duo rented their own room together and spent several nights from September 30 to October 7 together in that room.

A coworker saw Kristin at the conference during the week and noted that she was no longer wearing her wedding ring.

One of the conferences that Rossum and Robertson attended in Milwaukee was on the deadly effects of fentanyl. Fentanyl is a clear, odorless narcotic that is 100 times stronger than morphine. It is generally administered to cancer patients whose pain is not eased by other means. It is so potent that it only takes a few drops to kill.

The seminar also discussed the fact that the drug is so rarely prescribed and used that most medical examiner's offices do not test for it. Both Rossum and Robertson were well aware of the fact that their office did not test for fentanyl.

During the three years that Rossum had worked in the San Diego Medical Examiner's office, only seven cases of death by overdose had involved fentanyl. She had seen 15 patches and 1 vial of the drug in a powder form. It was Rossum's job to log and track the drugs in her logbook. It was Robertson's job to hold the key to the cabinet those substances was then stored in.

These were facts that seemed innocuous at the time but would soon hold a more serious meaning.

Returning to Old Ways

Only a day or two after returning from Milwaukee, Rossum sent de Villers an email telling him that she was taking three different prescription drugs "to help with the severe anxiety I've been experiencing as a result of our relationship. You've hurt me beyond repair."

Not only was Kristin taking prescription medications, she had fallen back into her addiction to meth. After some of the drugs went missing from her office, Robertson admitted later that he found traces of the drug in her desk and rather than turning his girlfriend in, he flushed the drugs down the toilet. Then he covered for her with his superiors.

Once again, Kristin Rossum has done something bad. Once again, somebody shields her from the ramifications of her actions. Once again, there are no consequences for Kristin's bad actions.

Severing Ties

By early November 2000, Rossum was ready to end her relationship with de Villers. She insisted she wanted only a "trial separation."

She later told detectives that de Villers literally collapsed when she told him she was leaving him. She claimed that he lay in bed for days afterward and would not communicate with her. She later told the court, "It was painful for me, too, to see someone you love hurt so much." She still never owned up to the fact that it was her own actions that caused her husband that pain.

On November 6, 2000, just after 9:15 pm, Kristin Rossum called 991.

She claimed that her husband was unresponsive and that she was doing CPR to try and revive him. When paramedics arrived, however, they found Rossum on the phone in the living room. Her husband was lying lifeless on their bed.

Gregory de Villers lay dead in his La Jolla bedroom with rose petals covering his chest. Besides his lifeless head lay a copy of his wedding picture ... less than two years old. Nearby on the floor lay a crumpled love letter from the dashing Australian doctor that was his wife's boss and lover. Beside that was his wife's discarded diary, open to an entry that she had left confiding that she felt her marriage was the biggest mistake of her life.

For all intents and purposes, it looked like a suicide. His distraught widow claimed that Greg had learned that her affair with Robertson was still happening.

However, de Villers' brother Jerome adamantly refused to accept that his brother had committed suicide. The entire de Villers family demanded an investigation. Still, the San Diego police were hesitant to open an investigation.

The Truth and Nothing but the Truth

Their opinion quickly changed and authorities soon came to suspect Kristin Rossum, de Villers' 26-year-old blonde beauty of a wife. They believed that she had used her knowledge as a toxicologist and the information that she had gleaned from working in the medical examiner's office to poison her husband.

Due to concerns over a conflict of interest, de Villers' autopsy was outsourced to another lab in Los Angeles. That lab is one of the few in the country that tests for fentanyl. They found 7 times the lethal dose of fentanyl in de Villers' system.

Two weeks after de Villers' death, the San Diego police brought Kristin Rossum in for interrogation. She reiterated to police that her husband had been extremely depressed.

According to Kristin Rossum's story, on the Thursday before de Villers' death, they struggled over a letter that she had sticking out of her back pocket. In her account, de Villers' attempted to grab the letter from her pocket and knocked her to the ground to wrest it from her. She claimed that it was the first time she had been afraid of her husband.

When he had the letter, as Rossum's story goes, he held it out and threatened to take it to his wife's office and expose the affair as well as her reoccurring meth addiction. She took the letter and shredded it but de Villers pieced it back together.

In court, Rossum's parents described the night, two days before de Villers' death, when they went over to visit the couple for dinner. Ralph Rossum testified that de Villers seemed to be deeply depressed, "a man spiraling down."

Kristin Rossum's father continued to describe how de Villers had drunk heavily that night. He drank wine and gin until his father in law had to tell him to lower his voice. Constance Rossum described Greg de Villers' voice as "fraught with melodrama" as he spoke at length about the dozen red roses that he had given to Kristin for her birthday a few days earlier.

She testified that he seemed depressed, agitated, and particularly obsessed with the fact that all but one had died and shed its petals. In a TV interview, she gave months after the death, Rossum stated, "He was making a big deal of the last rose standing. I think he was just making a statement that he knew our relationship was over."

Things rapidly spiraled from that point on. Police learned that Rossum had relapsed and was using meth again.

On June 25, 2001 – 7 months after Greg de Villers' death – his wife was arrested on charges of First Degree Murder. She spent over six months in jail and then on January 4, 2002, her parents posted $1.25 million for bail.

During the trial, the prosecution contended that she killed her husband to keep him from telling her bosses that she was having an affair with Robertson and that she was stealing meth from the office. They presented evidence that she had the knowledge about fentanyl to use it, access to the drug (remember the missing fentanyl from her office), and the motive to kill her husband.

On November 12, 2002, Kristin Rossum was found guilty of first-degree murder.

Exactly one month later on December 12, she was sentenced to life in prison without the chance of parole. She was transferred from the San Diego jail to the Central California Women's Facility in Chowchilla California – the largest women's correctional facility in the United States.

Distant Repercussions

In 2006, the de Villers family filed a lawsuit against Rossum and San Diego County for wrongful death. They were asking for $50 million but on March 25, 2006, a San Diego jury ordered Rossum to pay more than $100 million in punitive damages to the de Villers family. The same judge ordered San Diego County to pay $1.5 million.

According to the de Villers' lawyer John Gomez, the punitive damages awarded in this case are the most assessed against an individual defendant in California history. The jury apparently awarded double what the de Villers' family was asking for due to the estimation that Rossum could make $60 million from selling the rights to her story.

The judge later lowered the awarded amounts to $10 million in punitive damages and $4.5 million in a compensatory award.

In September of 2010, a 3-judge panel of the 9th US Circuit Court of Appeals ruled that Rossum's lawyers should have challenged the prosecutions assertion that she poisoned her husband with fentanyl by demanding their own tests. Due to this, the panel ordered a San Diego federal court to hold a hearing into whether the defense's error could have affected the trial's outcome.

On September 13, 2011, the US Court of Appeals withdrew its opinion and replaced it with a one-paragraph statement that denied Rossum's petition.

Conclusion

Kristin Rossum will spend the rest of her life behind bars. She has exhausted her state appeals and the federal courts denied her petition to be heard.

Her contention remains that her husband killed himself. She further believes that he did it the way that he did to point the finger of guilt at her. She vehemently insists that she did not kill her husband.

At one point, Kristin Rossum even suggested that her lover the handsome Australian doctor might have killed her husband. He knew about de Villers' threat to expose them before his death and had access to the fentanyl.

For his part, Robertson returned to Brisbane, Australia only one month after de Villers' death under the excuse that he had to care for his ailing mother. In September of 2013, the San Diego Reader reported that prosecutors filed a criminal complaint against Robertson in 2006 charging him with one count of conspiracy to obstruct justice.

If he returned to the US, Robertson could face up to three years in prison. In 2001, Robertson was named as an "unindicted co-conspirator" in Rossum's trial.

As of 2014, Robertson was running a forensic consulting business in Brisbane.

Kristin Rossum, the sweet spoiled only daughter of college professors, who was never held accountable for her actions as she grew up will spend the rest of her days within the walls of the largest women's correctional facility in the US. She is finally going to have to answer for what she has done.

BLACK WIDOW LYDA TRUEBLOOD

JESSI DILLARD

A true "black widow"

Death followed Lyda Trueblood everywhere she went. At first glance, it may have seemed that the young woman was facing a run of bad luck – but as the run continued, suspicions began to arise.

Northeast of Kansas City, in the small town of Keytesville, Missouri, a true "black widow" was born on October 16, 1892. Over the course of her life, Lyda Anna Mae Trueblood took on seven married names, and is most well-known as Lyda Southard. However, Idaho remembers her as Lady Bluebeard – the state's first female serial killer.

"She swept the men of her choice off their feet – courted them so persistently that they could not escape," said V. H. Ormsby, a deputy sheriff from Twin Falls, Idaho. Ormsby was one of the officers who arrested Trueblood in Honolulu for the death of her fourth husband.

By the age of 27, Trueblood had already killed six people, including her own daughter. However, she would only be convicted of one murder – the poisoning of her fourth husband, Edward Meyer, in 1921.

"The marital experiences of the one-time Missouri country town girl eclipses even those of fiction. Ten years ago, while still in her teens, she was attending Sunday school and enjoying the popularity that goes with being a village belle."

Described as "pudgy faced and plain of figure," Trueblood still caught the eye of Robert Dooley, whose family was close with Trueblood's. Some said Trueblood was the most popular girl at her high school, claiming she had an "indefinable something, a spark giving off a light that draws men, by physiological and chemical attraction."

"They wasn't so wealthy, just so-so," said Mrs. Larrabee Hanson, who lived near the Trueblood family. "But they were all church-going people, devout and clean-living. (Trueblood) went to church every Sunday without fail."

A magazine writer, Alan Jaffe, who detailed Trueblood's history for a profile in *Argosy* magazine in 1957, said men "hung around her like flies about a honey pot." In fact, when Trueblood finally left her childhood home and moved to Twin Falls, Robert Dooley followed – and the two were married there in 1912, when she was only 21.

A promise of the future

"They had a perfectly normal relationship," said Mychel Matthews with the Twin Falls County Historical Museum. "They appeared to be just like the rest of the residents around town."

With the security of their future family in mind, the newlyweds decided to take out an insurance policy on Robert and his brother, Edward. If either died, the survivor would inherit $1,000 – with an equal amount going to Trueblood. And by August 1915, the couple was $2,000 richer. Edward Dooley had fallen ill and had died after just a few days – typhoid, the doctors said.

"There was nothing suspicious about the death," Matthews said. "It was ruled as food poisoning or typhoid."

As Edward lay dying, Trueblood convinced her husband to revise his insurance policy – for the family's protection, she argued. A new policy was drafted for Robert and his wife, stating that if either died, the surviving spouse would receive $2,000.

Just one month later, Robert Dooley followed in his brother's footsteps – succumbing to typhoid in a similar fashion. Trueblood, however, had begun to build herself a substantial nest egg. Only six weeks after losing her husband, Trueblood's infant daughter, Laura Marie, "drank from a contaminated well," according to reports – leaving the widow lonely and desperate for companionship.

Since accidental poisonings did occasionally occur in rural areas, and epidemics – particularly typhoid – were rampant during that time, the deaths of the Dooleys were only briefly investigated by authorities.

"Little children died all the time, at that period of history," Matthews said. "She probably got a lot of sympathy, 'oh, that poor woman. She's lost her daughter, her husband, all to this stomach flu.'"

Trueblood endured a brief but mandatory period of mourning after losing her family, but soon struck up a relationship with a waiter at her favorite Twin Falls restaurant. William McHaffie married Trueblood just two years after the loss of her first husband and only child, and the couple immediately sought an insurance policy for William. Trueblood was named as William's only beneficiary, to receive $5,000 if anything was to happen to him.

The couple moved to Hardin, Montana, and only a year after they married, William died of "influenza." According to his friends and customers, William had always been a robust, healthy man – and the speed and depth of his sudden illness shocked them.

"Lyda Trublood was very careful," said crime author Diane Fanning. "She waited until they actually got sick – then, it was easier to believe that they had died of an illness. Everybody thought it was something he ate that finally did him in, but all that it was, really, was Lyda Trueblood."

Unfortunately for Trueblood, however, William had failed to pay the second premium on his insurance policy, letting it lapse. Trueblood received nothing for her efforts. Days after her late husband's funeral, Trueblood sold all her property and disappeared.

Moving on

After relocating to Denver, Trueblood managed to ensnare another victim – a farm machinery salesman she had met during her previous marriage to William. In fact, William had told friends that after he'd come to their door in an attempt to make a sale, Trueblood had seemed "struck" by him – and neighbours reported that the happy couple had even started fighting more after that.

Trueblood married Harlan Lewis in March of 1919, and took him with her back to Montana. The couple settled in Billings, and only one month later, Harlan took out a $10,000 life insurance policy. According to Matthews, the larger policies are an indication that

Trueblood was manipulating the men in order to receive greater payouts.

"(Trueblood) was motivated by one thing, and one thing only - greed," said former FBI profiler Candice Delong. "She wanted money."

By mid-July, just three months after the wedding, disaster had struck. After falling ill to a sudden case "ptomaine poisoning," Harlan left Trueblood a widow for the third time – and this time, the cheque came through. After cashing out the estate, Trueblood disappeared again. Instead of heading somewhere new, however, Trueblood decided to return to Idaho.

Under the name of Lyda McHaffie, Trueblood checked into the Rogerson Hotel in Twin Falls in May 1919, and found herself a job at the Grille Café on Main Avenue. Business at the café picked up immediately, reports claim, and the foreman of Ira Perrine's Blue Lake Ranch, Edward Meyer, started visiting the restaurant regularly.

"Folks couldn't help noticing that the air sort of shimmered when (Trueblood's) eyes met Ed's," wrote Jaffe in his profile. "And that the ham he got was thicker, the eggs sunnier than those served other patrons."

The very next month, Trueblood moved to Pocatello, Idaho, where she married Edward Meyer and settled on a ranch.

"She rigged herself out fit to kill, bought a long mink coat and a closed car. Everybody in town was talking about the way she ran around to dances," said Ormsby. "She talked around town that she wasn't in love with Ed, but she wanted a home, and she said that sometime she might learn to love him."

Although she had started going by the name "Anna McHaffie," Trueblood showed no other signs of leaving her past life behind her. She applied for an insurance policy in Edward's name the day after the wedding, in the amount of $10,000 – however, the policy was not approved, and reasons were never clarified. It's possible that insurance companies were beginning to wise up to the run of bad luck Trueblood had encountered.

Suspicious situation

Only two weeks after the couple had wed, on August 25, Edward took ill. Doctors at the hospital claimed he had an excellent chance of recovery, but he was dead by September 7.

"She didn't wait for him to get sick," said Matthews. "Maybe she grew impatient, and that was probably the mistake she made in all of this."

Trueblood's previous husbands had been fairly low-key, unlikely to attract attention despite the unbelievable series of coincidences that had resulted in their deaths – and Trueblood's subsequent insurance claims. Edward Meyer, however, was a different case. As a prominent figure in Twin Falls, Edward had dealings with many of the leading business and farm people in the region – including the Twin Falls county sheriff.

"The townsfolk weren't just satisfied," Ormsby said. "They started a lot of talk, and the insurance company held up payment on the policy. The matter got into politics and folks wanted to know what the candidates for sheriff would do about (Trueblood)."

When traces of arsenic were discovered during a routine post-mortem examination, detectives finally brought the widow in for questioning.

"The investigation was just getting underway when the woman disappeared," stated an article published in the New York Times on May 13, 1921. "Detectives traced her to Los Angeles, and kept track of her while the bodies of the two (Dooleys), the infant daughter, and McHaffie were exhumed and portions of the viscera were sent to chemists."

Edward Meyer's death had become somewhat of a political issue in the 1920 campaign for sheriff, and potential candidates were asked how they planned to handle the case. The current sheriff passed the case to a "remarkable" deputy, Virgin Ormsby – and the investigation would be virtually his only assignment for months.

"After she left for California, the town got more dissatisfied than ever, and in January, I was assigned to the case," Ormsby said. "I've had the bodies of the men dissatisfied and examined – three chemists each working separately reported to me that they found arsenic. I interviewed the doctors who attended the husbands and obtained statements from them that enabled me to build a strong case against her."

Ormsby even discovered that a relative of Trueblood's first husband and brother-in-law had been studying the suspicious deaths in his family. A chemist named Earl Dooley had already begun to consider the possibility that Robert and Edward Dooley had been poisoned with arsenic – and according to Fanning, his suspicions led him to investigate the scene of Trueblood's most recent victim.

After taking samples from Edward Meyer's vomit in the sand, Earl had them tested.

"Sure enough, he found arsenic – and when that happened, he went to a doctor to get it confirmed in another lab," Fanning said. "It was definitely arsenic."

Mounting evidence

Police first determined that the Dooley brothers had been poisoned, as well as Trueblood's own child. Officers in Montana started investigating the cases of Harlan Lewis and William McHaffie, intrigued by the seemingly impossible coincidences that had led Trueblood to make so many insurance claims. Trueblood, meanwhile, was busy seducing her fifth husband, Paul Southard, in Los Angeles – while prosecutor Frank L. Stephen started building a case against her back in Twin Falls.

While working odd jobs, saving her money, and reportedly describing herself as a nurse, Trueblood managed to convince Paul to propose. The two were married in November of 1920. Although Paul, who served as a seaman in the navy, claimed he needed no additional insurance coverage beyond typical provisions, Ormsby learned that a policy had in fact been taken out on Chief Petty Officer Paul Southard – with Trueblood named as the beneficiary.

Shortly after they were wed, Paul was transferred from Los Angeles to Pearl Harbour, and his new bride joined him in Hawaii. Ormsby was in hot pursuit, having tracked Trueblood with the help of California law enforcement. Officers in Honolulu received a warrant for Trueblood's arrest in May 1921. She was picked up on May 12 to return to Boise, Idaho, for her trial – with her husband Paul at her side.

"She's been a mighty good wife to me," said Paul, who refused to believe the charges, "and I don't care if she married ten men before, and they all died. That wouldn't make her a murderess."

Although tabloids had already started running headlines about the gruesome tale, labelling Trueblood catchy names like "Lethal Lyda" or "The Arsenic Widow," Trueblood maintained her innocence as she and Paul prepared to catch the *Matsonia* out of Honolulu. Some reports claimed she was acting "like any lucky vacationer about to embark on an ocean cruise," her neck heavy with flowered leis.

"I am entirely innocent, and I look forward to the trip with optimism," Trueblood said in a brief statement to the press. "I am anxious to get back to Twin Falls and face my accusers."

At the jail, Trueblood finally granted an interview to reporter Hazel Pedlar Faulkner, with the San Francisco Examiner. Pedlar Faulkner described the accused as "dainty, friendly, and refined" – not exactly the picture of a "sinister murderer," she said.

"I have been nervous because of my imprisonment and the unnecessary disgrace to my husband," Pedlar Faulkner quotes Trueblood as saying. "I know as well as anything that I can clear myself. The evidence gathered against me is purely circumstantial. Their work is to prove the charges, and that will not be easy because of the documents I hold."

Trueblood claimed that her husbands had died because she was a "typhoid carrier," and even stated that she had nothing to do with the large life insurance policies her late husbands had all secured before their untimely deaths.

"Life insurance was no object to me," stated Trueblood in Pedlar Faulkner's interview. "I have had enough money. And what insurance my husbands carried were business propositions they took out without regard to me or without consulting me, generally."

Before leaving San Francisco to bring Trueblood back to Boise, Ormsby and his wife, Nellie, took the accused for one last night on the town. After having dinner at a restaurant and strolling through a downtown shopping district, the Ormsbys and their charge attended a vaudeville show at the Orpheum Theatre.

Although Trueblood was trying to remain under the radar, a San Francisco Chronicle reporter recognized her – and wrote about her activities the next morning.

"With the grim specters of four dead husbands, a brother-in-law, and her infant baby hovering near her, while the accusing finger of the law points at her and charges murder, Mrs. Lyda Eva Southard, psychological enigma, calmly spent yesterday seeing the sights of San Francisco," read Herb Westen's article in the San Francisco Call and Post.

"She smiles, a trifle shyly perhaps, but a bored light creeps around her eyes as if to her it is all a tedious legal jumble, which will steal precious hours from her pursuit of happiness."

Up to the jury

Despite Trueblood's denial of the charges, the state contended that she'd fed Edward Meyer, her fourth husband, hefty doses of arsenic extracted from flypaper. Trueblood denied it and the state presented further evidence – largely circumstantial, but it was still enough for a conviction.

The trial, which started on October 3 and lasted six weeks, received attention nation-wide. At the time, it would become the longest criminal trial in history. Witnesses were called from Missouri, Montana, Tennessee, and California – a total of 182 named to appear, but not all were called to the stand.

Prosecutor Stephen tried desperately to bring in Buddy Thornberg to testify against Trueblood – a reporter for the Daily News in Twin Falls who had come close to marrying Trueblood shortly before she snagged Edward Meyer. He'd met the widow at the café, and she had swept him off his feet. According to reports, Thornberg had told his friends he would be marrying the "rich widow from Montana," and – on her advice – he was considering taking out an additional private insurance policy on top of the $10,000 government policy he already had in place.

After his friends managed to convince him to not follow through with a marriage, however, Thornberg had ended his relationship with Trueblood and was presumed to have moved to Washington – never to be heard from again.

An article claimed that "every session of the trial found the court auditorium filled to capacity, principally by women and girls." Another report claimed the trail was, "draggy," and "rather technical – arsenic versus typhoid, laboratory tests versus the official death certificate. This certificate, giving typhoid as the cause of death, was more or less (Trueblood's) sole defense."

The whole case presented against Trueblood suggested that she didn't particularly love her husband, and could have – and likely did – poison him. Not only that, she took out insurance on his life, and fled immediately after his death.

According to Ormsby, a visit to the McHaffies' home in Montana had uncovered evidence to back up this theory. He'd discovered a "large quantity" of cut-up flypaper containing arsenic in the basement, with residue of arsenic in a pot Trueblood had likely used to boil the poison out – before serving it to her husband in tainted food.

"(Trueblood) went about her killing very deliberately," Fanning said. "She bought out everything the store had in flypaper. It was obvious that she wanted to have a permanent supply on hand."

An article published in the New York Times on October 9, 1921 stated that under the questioning of Prosecuting Attorney Frank Stephen, Dr E. F. Roberbaugh, state chemist, confirmed the presence of arsenic poison in the body of Edward Meyer when he examined the body in April of that year.

"The witness testified he found .05 milligrams of poison in five grams of a specimen of several internal organs and .10 milligrams in a ten-gram quantity of the specimen," the article read. "The witness said the distribution of poison throughout the system was not equal and he estimated that a little less than five grains of poison probably was contained in Meyer's body."

He added that the findings "virtually duplicated" those obtained immediately after Edward Meyer's death in September, 1920.

The state requested permission to introduce further evidence relating to the deaths of Trueblood's other husbands, and the judge ruled the testimony admissible. While physicians did, in some instances, contradict testimony of other expert witnesses on the question of cause of death, analysis made by three separate chemists agreed that poison was present in all bodies exhumed.

"She poisoned their food, and over time, the arsenic would build up," said Fanning. "Most of the death certificates all said some sort of stomach ailment."

After a deliberation of twenty-three hours, the jury came back with a verdict on November 4, 1921. Trueblood was found guilty of second-degree murder. Speculation was that the jury had "blanched" at the thought of hanging a woman, but there was no doubt that she had done it. Even her husband, Paul Southard, filed for divorce after watching the trial.

"Lyda Trueblood was a classic black widow," Delong said. "And she did it for money."

According to an article in the November 5, 1921 issue of the Sacramento Union, Trueblood showed "no sign of feeling," and didn't even raise her eyes from the floor as the verdict was read. This was typical of Trueblood's attitude throughout the trial, however.

"On the stand, the accused woman maintained an unperturbed attitude throughout a long grilling by the prosecution, which failed to adduce any important admissions from her," the article stated.

Only eight years after Trueblood's incarceration, Ormsby suffered a paralytic stroke and died in his wife's arms. His obituary ran on the front page of the December 30, 1929 edition of the Twin Falls Times – and flowers were delivered to his funeral, sent from a Lyda Southard.

A "break for freedom"

Still, the guilty verdict and the sentence of at least ten years in prison wasn't enough to keep Trueblood from seducing men.

"She proved that no prison walls can hold her, and made her escape from the Idaho State Penitentiary by fascinating, as did Milady, a prison guard, who is believed to have rigged up for her an ingenious ladder of plumbers' pipes and torn blankets and garden hose," read an article published in the October 25, 1931 issue of the Salt Lake Tribune. "This guard, however, died before (Trueblood) made her break for freedom."

According to the article, Trueblood had already served ten years of her sentence and was eligible for parole when she made her great escape on May 4, 1931. The ladder, fashioned for her by prison guard Jack Watkins, had been buried for months beneath the prison walls. Watkins had also provided Trueblood with a saw, which she used to remove a bar from her cell window.

"The escape itself was dramatic," the article continued. "Women inmates, evidently under the spell of the woman, who could fascinate those of her own sex as well as men, staged a party and played the phonograph and sang while she was gaining her way to liberty."

Trueblood ran right into the arms of David Minton. Minton, an ex-convict himself, had fallen under Trueblood's spell while he was still behind bars. After he helped Trueblood escape from prison, she'd ended the relationship. Leaving him alive was a mistake, however – enraged, Minton went to the police and told them they could find Trueblood in Topeka, Kansas.

This, however, was not before a nation-wide manhunt was organized to attempt to locate Trueblood, who was described by Warden R. E. Thomas of the Idaho State Penitentiary as "one of the most dangerous criminals at large."

"Some man will probably pay with his life in agony and death before this ruthless woman can again be brought to justice," he said. "That she is the modern 'Mrs. Bluebeard' is certain."

In fact, before the police found her in Kansas, Trueblood had managed to swindle another man into marrying her. Harry Whitlock, who later described Trueblood as a "model wife," was shocked when the police showed up looking for her. The relationship had begun when Trueblood, calling herself "Fern," had started doing housekeeping work for Whitlock – and she had suggested he take out a $20,000 life insurance policy, but it hadn't been purchased before she asked him for some travel money and took off.

Fifteen months after her escape, Trueblood was returned to Boise – with her marriage to Whitlock annulled.

Back in prison, Trueblood continued to seduce her prey. This time, she set her sights on George Rudd, a prison warden. She managed to convince him to grant her special privileges – frequent day trip to a local resort, visitation to see her sick mother, and even transportation to Boise to see movies. However, when authorities discovered that he'd been treating Trueblood to these privileges, Rudd was forced to resign from his position.

Free at last

Finally, Trueblood was paroled from prison on October 3, 1941, and fully pardoned only one year later.

"I think they figured that she had lost most of her good looks and charm, and was no longer a menace to society," Matthews said.

After spending a few years living with her sister, Blanche Quigley, in Nyssa, Oregon, Trueblood returned to her family's farm at Twin Falls – but the local townspeople and even her relatives weren't pleased to see her.

A few months later, Trueblood left for Provo, Utah, where no one knew her, and pulled together the funds to purchase a small secondhand shop. There, she married her seventh husband, Hal Shaw. However, once Shaw's children discovered who she was and learned about her unsavory past, he vanished – leaving her to move to Salt Lake City, where she worked for several years as a housekeeper and waitress.

"You wonder, did (the husbands) ever suspect that it was not a natural illness that was making them suffer in agony," Fanning said. "We can only hope that they never understood what was really happening."

Trueblood died of a heart attack on February 5, 1958 in Salt Lake City. Her body remains at Sunset Memorial Park in Twin Falls, Idaho, where she was buried as Anna E. Shaw. Still, some report seeing a ghost bearing Trueblood's likeness haunting the halls of the Idaho prison to this day – the prison's most notorious inmate, maintaining a presence even after her death.

"When she finally died, it was from a heart attack," Fanning said. "It's amazing to think that (Trueblood) actually had a heart."

BLACK WIDOW : THE TRUE STORY OF MARGARET RUDIN

BRIANNA VALDES

Margaret Rudin, dubbed the Black Widow of Las Vegas, went on trial on February 26, 2001 for the murder of her fifth husband, real estate king Ronald Rudin. After a lengthy, chaotic trial and her defense claiming that involvement in illegal activities resulted in Ron's death, the jury found her guilty on May 2, 2001. In August, the court sentenced Margaret Rudin to life in prison with the possibility of parole in 20 years.

According to reports, Ron Rudin went missing about a week before Christmas in '94. He paid a visit to wife Margaret Rudin's antique shop, in the same plaza as his real estate business. Officials said that Margaret Rudin did not report Ron missing until a few days after he disappeared. She told police she thought nothing of it at first because, aside from Ron being upset with her after an argument, he seemed like his usual self.

About a month after Ron disappeared, a couple of civilians stumbled upon human remain near Lake Mohave in Nevada. Police found ashes and fragments of bones in the burn pile. However, the skull, which was inches away, remained mostly intact. It had at least four bullet holes, which forensics later matched to a .22 caliber weapon. Police made two trips to the house, and on the second visit, they found blood on the walls, photographs and items removed from the house including a mattress and carpet. However, though the police suspected that Margaret Rudin killed her husband, the evidence up to that point was circumstantial at best.

A year and a half year later, a diver found a .22 caliber gun with a built-in silencer in Lake Mead. This was the same gun Ron Rudin reported missing about six years before his death. When officials tested the gun in the forensics lab, the ammo matched the rounds found in Ron Rudin's skull. Police determined that the .22 was the murder weapon, and, with this new piece of evidence added to the other circumstantial clues they had, charged Margaret Rudin with the murder of her husband. However, Margaret left town before they indicted and arrested her, and she stayed out of sight for over two years.

Almost a year after the diver found the gun that allegedly killed Ron Rudin, police finally indicted Margaret Rudin.

Authorities finally apprehended Margaret Rudin in 1999. Someone who saw her picture and story on the T.V. show "America's Most Wanted" called and reported seeing her in a small town in Massachusetts.

Police used a pizza delivery person to help them capture Margaret. They borrowed the person's uniform and an empty pizza box, and barged in the house when her male companion opened the door. According to some reports, they found her cowering in the bathroom.

Margaret Rudin was born Margaret Lee Frost in Memphis, Tennessee on May 31, 1943. She said that she and her family never lived in one place for very long, and that she and her two sisters constantly changed schools.

"I didn't grow up any place. We were constantly moving, you know, like, I transferred schools 22 different times, um, before I graduated high school. I lived in 15 states in 15 years. I never had a hometown."

Margaret said that her father was strict and dominating, and that he rarely showed affection to her or her sisters.

Both Margaret and Ron were married four times before they met at the First Church of Religious Science in Las Vegas. They married on September 11, 1987.

Margaret's mother, Eloise Frost, stood behind her daughter throughout the entire trial. She never believed Margaret capable of murder.

"I want to live long enough to see Margaret pronounced innocent, because she is innocent."

Margaret Rudin's daughter, Kristina Mason firmly believed that her mother was innocent. She said her childhood was a good one, and that the mother with whom she grew up was not a murderer.

"She's just a wonderful person and I'm proud to say she's my mother."

The court sentenced Margaret Rudin in September 2001. Although she received life in a medium security facility, plus a year for planting the bugs in her husband's office, they also added that she would be eligible for parole in 2011. She began preparing, and petitioning, for her appeal, carefully heeding the filing deadlines.

80-year-old Eloise cried when Margaret was convicted, saying that now she may never see her daughter again.

Kristina Mason burst into tears.

"I'm so disappointed."

Ronald Rudin seemed to predict his own death, or at least his murder. Months before he went missing, he had his will changed, with specific instructions for investigators to follow in the event that he died under suspicious circumstances.

"In the event my death is caused by violent means [for example gunshot, knife or a violent automobile accident] extraordinary steps be taken in investigating the true cause of the death. Should said death be caused directly or indirectly by a beneficiary of my estate, said beneficiary shall be totally excluded from my estate and/or any trusts I may have in existence."

Although most of Nevada's case against Margaret was circumstantial, authorities say there were a few things that seemed suspicious to them from the beginning. First, Margaret herself admitted that her marriage to Ron was less than ideal. She told police that they often argued about her work schedule. Later, when authorities discovered that she had planted listening devices in Ron Rudin's home office, she also admitted that she suspected that Ron was having an affair, and upon eavesdropping on a phone conversation, discovered proof to back her suspicions.

Jimmy Vacarro, a Vegas detective, confirmed that the Las Vegas police believed without a doubt that Margaret Rudin was responsible for Ron's murder.

"We know there was this real rocky roller-coaster relationship between Margaret Rudin and her husband... [It took] Margaret two days to file a missing persons report and that she did so only after Ron's coworkers informed police first...Generally speaking, the spouse is missing, the wife's the one reporting it."

Second, officials say that Margaret waited a few days before reporting Ron missing, even though his employees at his real estate company were concerned and investigating as soon as he did not show up that Monday morning.

Margaret Rudin offered a logical explanation to her hesitation to bring in police. She said she thought little of it at first because they had another fight and he left angry, which was common for Ron. She also said that, aside from Ron being upset with her after an argument, he seemed like his usual self.

"He seemed ok. He does not seem upset. He had, had been a little peeved at me over the weekend because I had to work all the time... "Well, I thought nothing of it because, you know, maybe he did get peeved... and maybe he did decide to go out for awhile... maybe he did go to, you know... wherever."

Margaret made a point of mentioning her previous marriages in one of her interviews.

“I don't have a history of staying with somebody if I'm really unhappy. I have a history of divorcing... There was problems. He was a difficult person at times, but yes, I did love him...”

Margaret said Ron also drank quite a bit after just a few months of marriage. However, she told reporters that she was not mad about the alcohol or the other women, even when Su Lyles, a close friend and a former employee of Mr. Rudin's, testified that in the fall of 1993, their relationship became more intimate. At least twice, she said, they had discussed their feelings for each other over the telephone during calls made from his office.

"You know why? It is because 99 percent of the men that I have ever had in my life had affairs. Ninety percent of men do, you might as well expect it."

Margaret admitted that, although the affairs wounded her, she loved her husband and desperately wanted to work out things with him.

Police grew even more suspicious when they discovered that Margaret hired a man named Augustine Lovato to help her remove some dirty carpet and furniture from the master bedroom. She then renovated the bedroom she shared with her husband into an office while Ron was still missing.

Lovato testified that the mattress and carpet he removed from the Rudin’s home had suspicious brown stains on it and a strong odor that alarmed him.

"It didn't seem right, him still being missing and me turning their master bedroom into an office and then those splatters on that picture. Like I got the heebie-jeebies."

Lovato also claimed that he heard a strange sound in the bathtub in the master bathroom. He said that, upon inspection, it looked about the same color and consistency as the stains on the mattress and carpet he removed.

The same day he moved the allegedly bloodstained items from the Rudin's bedroom, Margaret Rudin asked Lovato to mail a package addressed to her mother. Lovato claimed that he forgot to mail the package, and ultimately turned it over to the police. After obtaining a search warrant, police opened the package and discovered several personal items inside, including a postcard from Israel signed "Love, Yehuda," a photo of Yehuda Sharon, the man with whom police suspected that Margaret Rudin was having an affair, and a handwritten letter from Rudin to her mother containing the message, "Please hold on to my Ye."

Attorneys discovered later that Lovato reported all these mysterious findings after Ron Rudin's other trustees announced their reward for information about Ron's disappearance. However, Lovato argued that he cooperated with police before anyone told him there was a reward, which Ron's trustees did grant him.

The most suspicious thing that Margaret Rudin did, according to police, was going on the run before the state served her with her indictment. Investigators believed that, if Margaret were innocent, she would not have fled. However, Margaret says that she ran out of fear, not guilt.

"[I ran] because I was afraid of being found by Ron's shadowy business associates... It was difficult. I was always looking over my shoulder. I was always afraid, I was afraid of who stood to gain the most, you know, from Ron's murder."

During the trial, the state also used the testimony of almost 70 witnesses, including Yehuda Sharon and Margaret's sister, Donna Cantrell. Prosecutors granted Yehuda Sharon total immunity in exchange for his testimony against Margaret Rudin. However, when he took the stand, he not only had little to say regarding Margaret's guilt, he denied aiding her in disposing of Ron Rudin's remains. He told the court that he rented a van, planning to make a trip from Vegas to California for his business on the night in question. However, he said that he only made it half way there and then turned around due to unexpected weather conditions. Furthermore, his destination was the opposite direction from the place where officials found Ron Rudin's remains. Once the prosecution determined that Margaret's friend, Yehuda Sharon, was likely not an accomplice to Ron's murder, no other suspects were detained or questions, and most people assumed that Margaret had somehow dismembered her husband's body, put it in the heavy steamer trunk and hauled it out to the desert all by herself.

Cantrell testified that she was aware of her sister's marital problems. She said that Margaret had spoken to her many times about Ron's drinking and her suspicions about his involvement with other women. She made comments on Rudin's restless desire to get away from Ron.

"I said, 'I thought you were going to divorce him,' and she said, 'He's not in very good health. He can't even walk without being out of breath, and I think I'll wait.' [Margaret told me] to tell [police] that she and Ron were getting along better than ever. And that the girlfriend wasn't an issue. [I don't] think that this statement would have been true."

Despite the authorities' strong belief that she murdered her husband, Margaret Rudin maintained her innocents. In interviews after the trial and her conviction, she states repeatedly that she loved her husband and could never kill him. She suggested that there might be another motive for her husband's murder.

"Nobody knows the whole Ron. That's the part that worries me. Maybe there's something that was going on with a business or a personal deal."

Margaret also suspected that someone knew more than they told detectives.

"I think that there are people that know things. I think that there are people who haven't come forth before. Maybe they didn't know how, maybe they were afraid, maybe they were intimidated."

Margaret Rudin's trial was rocky from the beginning. One of her defense attorneys, Michael Amador, started with an opening statement, which consisted of nothing but a long, irrelevant, self-based speech.

"This is a great day, in a lot of different ways. Some days are difficult; some days we hear bad news or we go through a difficult time, but every day, every day, depending on how you look at it, with a few exceptions, can be a celebration.

This is a great today for me. This is a culmination of a career. The people in this case, we are not strangers; we know each other. Chris and I were sworn in as deputy DAs the same day. And I congratulate Chris on a presentation that was organized and well thought out, the best money can buy. It was really good.

If you want to know an opinion about me, I guarantee you'll find some, different ones from different people. Not many people know me. I have few close friends, like Ronald Rudin had few close friends.

I could be a wonderful, caring father, coaching soccer, helping kids with their homework, which I did the first time I got married when they were young.

Then another day, I might scream at someone, yell at them for-I don't know-for asking me some question, because I was too busy and I was thinking of something else.

The difficulty I have at times is communicating to people. I have to look at it and talk to other people and they will bring me back down to earth and say, Mike, what are you trying to say? What are you trying to get across?"

Amador also made a strange, challenging statement.

"During the course of the trial, there may be objections and things like that. Don't worry about it."

Judge Joseph Bonaventure cut off Amador's speech.

"I don't know what that means: Don't worry about objections. We have to do other things. I have no idea what that means. If there's an objection, I'm either going to overrule it or sustain it and that's the law...

I keep saying this-and I let you get away with a lot, Mr. Amador-but the purpose for an opening statement is just to indicate what the evidence is going to tend to show and not go into your personal beliefs and your passion and soccer dad and yelling at the staff and whether you were a green lawyer and know all the cops and used to be a D.A. and you communicate differently. I never heard that in [an] opening statement in my life."

During the opening statements, the State quoted a portion of Margaret Rudin's diary.

"My life has always been unique, exciting, full of change, challenges and stimulus and full of interesting casts of characters and that is okay.

It just is, and I accept that for my past, but I know that, by programming my mind, I can now redirect any future stage plays and pick my own screen play and cast, because I am the producer, director and star of any and all new plays on my stage called life.

I've always vaguely known these facts and lived my life accordingly, but I never realized what control-I never realized what control I could have over every segment of this one time stage production called "Margaret's Life.""

Amador did a curious thing at the trial. He employed a makeup artist from a professional modeling agency and paid almost $500 an hour, out of his own pocket, to make Margaret appear worn, delicate, and tired.

Amador got under Judge Bonaventure's skin by repeatedly being late to appear in court, questionable forms he submitted, and his cell phone, which he never turned off or down during the trial. Rumors eventually spread that Amador was using drugs, drinking and partying all night long when he had to be in court early the next morning.

Rumors circulated that Amador was also behaving inappropriately with Margaret Rudin's belongings and private, confidential information. Amador hired a new office assistant named Annie Jackson during the proceedings for the Rudin trial. She revealed information regarding some of the rumors about Amador.

"There is no other way to say the following: when Mr. Amador told the court that he did not have any book or movie contracts, he was lying. Michael Amador does have book contracts and movie contracts regarding the Margaret Rudin case. When we returned to the office after Mr. Amador made those false representations to the court, he asked me to grab all of the contracts so that he could put them in his little safe in the back closet. He told me, "I don't want anyone to find out that I have these, then I'm sure they'll be investigating and looking for these."

Margaret asked early on for an even amount of participation from her attorneys. She asked that Thomas Pitaro take a more active role in the proceedings, because she did not believe that Michael Amador was properly prepared.

"We haven't even subpoenaed my witnesses yet. And I'm getting so nervous. I mean, I'm getting panicky."

Pitaro agreed after warning the judge that, although he would do his best, he was uncertain if he would be able to uphold that bargain throughout the entire trial.

Throughout all the chaos in the Rudin trial, one juror believed Margaret's side of the story. During the first couple of days of deliberation, she held fast to her opinion that Margaret did not kill Ron. However, hours before the foreperson read the jury's verdict, juror #11 changed her vote. She was distraught, wiping her eyes with a napkin. She hesitated before replying with a hushed "Yes" when the court asked her if the verdict was, in fact, hers, too.

Even though the verdict was ultimately unanimous, the juror cried as she apologized to Rudin when the foreperson read the jury's verdict.

During the time before she opted to vote Margaret Rudin guilty, juror #11 faced allegations from her peers of choosing not to join the deliberation efforts, lying, and calling one of the jury substitutes with her concerns about the case. Amador said he thought the juror was possibly "brow-beaten" into changing her vote.

Foreperson for the Rudin case's jury, Ronald Vest, said that no one "twisted her arm."

"We didn't bribe her or threaten her. She came to this on her own."

Vest believed that Rudin's was an open and shut case.

"Rudin's guilt was clear early on. [The defense's case was] a waste of time... [Amador was] bordering on incompetent... [The guilty verdict was a] slam dunk with a stepladder... I didn't buy any of it. I don't think any of us bought any of the defense case. The mountain of evidence had 11 of the jurors ready to convict as early as Thursday, but one person from the beginning did not see it that way... juror #11 seemed so bent on acquitting Rudin that [I] began to wonder if she had been bribed or threatened or simply wanted attention. [I] confronted her about [my] suspicions, and she denied them. There was a little bit of swearing. It was fast and furious but we hashed it out."

Vest admitted that he had had to request substitutes on a few occasions, because his special needs students were struggling in class without him. He believed that, had he not been there, they would not have been able to replace him.

"Six substitutes, three of which said they would never come back and one who just sat at the desk shaking like he was scared... my principal said, Well, maybe there's some reason why you need to be on this jury."

The judge in the Rudin trial met with the hesitant juror privately, in his chambers, to address her contact, and discussion about case-related information, with an alternate juror. Whenever Margaret Rudin's defense team broached the subject, the court dismissed it, stating that it had little impact on the outcome of the trial.

Margaret Rudin's conviction shocked Amador. He spoke with disdain about the prosecutors. He could not believe that the prosecutors successfully sold their case.

"If you have any understanding of psychology, history, or criminology, women don't do that, men do," said Amador. "That kind of mutilation is done by men over money or, in rare cases, serial killers. Women don't even order stuff like that—they want it clean... [The prosecutors] make me sick... I don't know how it is that right-thinking people can find someone guilty with no evidence."

Rudin had requested a mistrial due to Amador's antics and all the dissention with the jury. Pitaro led the defense team at the motion, hoping to prove that Amador was ill prepared for the case and not behaving with appropriate competence as an attorney.

"The fundamental problem that we have is this case is not ready to go to trial. For whatever reason it's not ready, it's not ready. That's obvious to any observer of this case, that for the first two weeks this is not the way you try cases and this is not the way you try murder cases. And what we are putting on in front of the world is a farce, and that disturbs me as an attorney. [T]his has become a sham, a farce and a mockery."

The State expressed similar concerns.

"Already we have an appellate issue now, should they have hired a forensic accountant. And I mean they came into this thing hiring their experts two weeks before the trial and they didn't start looking at the evidence until the day of trial. Two days into it, we still don't have reports back for most of them... Mr. Pitaro is coming in now, he's going to try to read the stuff and catch up. He already feels there's certain things that should have happened that didn't happen. All I can say is we're really uncomfortable with the record here."

The district court, however, was hesitant to declare a mistrial because of the double jeopardy laws. As it turned out, those did not apply in Margaret Rudin's case.

Amador stood with Margaret Rudin and the rest of her defense team during the motion for mistrial. However, when the prosecutors submitted documentation regarding his ineffectiveness, he contradicted himself.

"Nobody worked harder or spent more time before or during the Rudin trial nor knew the case better than I... [I] spend many hours on the case, from the time [I] took it in August of 2000 and [my] vacation in November 2000... [I] filed at least 24 motions and investigated all major witnesses in the case and organized their files prior to the vacation."

The defense also argued that improper communication took place between the judge, juror 11 and the alternate, which tainted the jury. According to the alternate, juror 11 called the alternate, saying she was upset because she was the only person in favor of a not guilty verdict and because she had gotten into an altercation with the staff person at a restaurant during a recess. After questioning the alternate and the juror in the presence of the State and the defense, the district court denied Rudin's motion for a mistrial. The district court also chose not to replace the juror. They concluded that neither the jury nor Rudin's case were compromised.

The court removed Amador from Margaret Rudin's case, but rejected her request for a mistrial. The judge almost immediately disregarded Margaret's mistrial motion.

"[Rudin] failed to present any specific argument to support a determination that she has been prejudiced. [The] affidavits are legally insufficient, as conclusions, rumors, beliefs, and opinions are not sufficient to form a basis for a new trial... As to Mr. Amador's personal antics which the defense seems to harp upon as tantalizing tidbits, this court feels it is not honorable to kick a man when he is down as the record speaks for itself. Rudin, at taxpayer expense, also had at her side criminal defense attorneys Thomas Pitaro and John Momot."

Bonaventure was biased, blunt, and cold at Margaret's sentencing hearing, just as he was throughout the entire trial.

"You're going to be locked away in the cold confines of your prison cell, never to be heard from again."

Although she received life in a medium security facility, plus a year for planting the bugs in her husband's office, they also added that she would be eligible for parole in 2011. She began preparing, and petitioning, for her appeal, carefully heeding the filing deadlines.

The appeals court believed that one of Margaret Rudin's former attorneys, Dayvid Figler, was responsible for her initial petitions for appeal. Figler denied any wrongdoing, and said that, although he was not at fault, she did deserve a shot at a new trial.

"I didn't screw up her trial. I didn't screw up her appeal. The court was giving extra time to get this very burdensome case before it. Everyone was operating under the assumption that she had more time to file the post-conviction appeal."

Figler called Rudin's appeal a "very complicated, burdensome, voluminous case" and said that after he took it on, the trial judge granted him extra time because the case was so complex.

Christopher Oram, the lawyer who represented Margaret Rudin during her recent appeal for a new trial, was thrilled with the opportunity.

"She is absolutely innocent. We've been working to prove it for a long time. I'm trying to reverse 10 years of complex litigation that was very unfair... I believe in her innocence. I'm ready to fight, and I wish they would stop playing their games. In the end, get in the ring and fight."

The Ninth Circuit Court of Appeals said that a technicality should not hinder Margaret Rudin's attempt to prove that a lawyer at her original trial ineffectually proved her case. Judge Mary Murguia believed that Figler did not serve Margaret to the best of his ability.

"While Figler regularly attended the court's status hearings, he appears to have done nothing else in support of his client's request for post-conviction relief. [Figler had the case for 645 days] and during that time, [he] had filed nothing in either state or federal court."

In 2007, Oram filed the first and only petition for post-conviction relief, according to Murguia.

Sally Loehrer, a district judge, ruled in 2008 that Michael Amador's performance did constitute as ineffectual in her original trial, and as a result, Margaret Rudin was entitled to a new trial.

"[It was a] case laced with intrigue and spins and loops involving a cast of characters and witnesses [that seemed to have] a lot of ulterior motives."

However, two years later, the Supreme Court overruled, stating that there was not enough evidence to sustain the order.

The Ninth Circuit Court reviewed all the evidence from the original trial, as well as Margaret Rudin's complaints, and her defense team's strategies. They do not believe that all defense attorneys adequately represent their clients just because they participate in every aspect of the trial. They made mention of evidence that was not previously mentioned.

"Sometime during the trial, the defense team located the person who sold the trunk to Rudin and established that it was not a large humpback trunk, but one that was much too small to fit a corpse inside. The defense also located Barbara Orcutt, who indicated that Rudin was indeed concerned about Ron's disappearance and had asked her right after his disappearance to organize a search in the Mt. Charleston area, where she believed Ron might have been. The State apparently had this information, but did not share it with the defense. It is unrealistic to think that the jurors could have put out of their minds all the evidence and adverse events, including the continual admonishment of defense counsel by the district court judge; the bizarre opening statement; the constant continuances and delays throughout the trial, which I am sure were held against the defense; and the belated presentation of important evidence. These harmful events resulted from Amador's conflict of interest and lack of preparation and now require reversal of this case... The evidence certainly indicated that Amador secured media rights while representing Rudin, which was a violation of the Nevada Rules of Professional Conduct.9...Amador was clearly more interested in obtaining information for his book and getting media attention than in developing Rudin's defense."

They also noted the testimony from Annie Jackson, Amador's assistant, and found new information there, as well. Jackson claimed that Amador did not turn over several of Rudin's files, containing diaries, witness statements, and pictures, to the public defender's office because he thought he might need the information in the future.

"I believe there is sufficient evidence in the record, without the necessity of post-trial proceedings, to establish that the defense was totally unprepared to try this case and that Amador had a substantial conflict of interest with his client. This was prejudicial to Rudin, and the result reached was unreliable."

Margaret appeals to the public in a letter she wrote from the Florence McClure Women's Correctional Center.

"The new trial I won [on] March 10, 2015, in the Ninth Circuit Court of Appeals has been blocked by the new NV Attorney General. Next week, their writ to the U.S. Supreme court will be filed."

She explains that, if her case lands in the 99% that skip review this session, it will return to the Ninth Circuit. Since they have already voted in her favor before, she hopes that once again, the NCCA will find her worthy of a new trial, and that this time their decision will be permanent. She maintains her innocence, and she continues to push for her appeal, and her opportunity to have her side of the story told.

HUSBAND KILLER : THE TRUE STORY OF MICHELLE HALL

TORI BAKER

It's never easy being a member of a blended family. There's a certain understanding that comes along with a second or third marriage – especially one involving children – that there is going to be a fundamental need for combined effort, tolerance and compromise.

When Michelle Garner remarried for what would be the third and last time, family and friends believed she had finally found happiness after reconnecting with an old high-school flame.

John Brittson "Britt" Hall, an aircraft mechanic and home builder, had known his own fair share of heartache; he was recently divorced when he found his old high school girlfriend, Michelle, on an online dating web site.

Britt Hall and Michelle Garner first met in 1986 while attending high school in Newnan, GA. The two briefly dated before Michelle Hall graduated in 1987.

"They both were in the popular clique," forensic psychologist Robert Brion said. "Britt was a baseball player that all of the girls had a crush on. Michelle was popular herself, very outgoing with a lot of friends."

The parents of Britt and Michelle were friends as well but they didn't consider the dating relationship between Michelle and Britt to be a serious one. After graduation, Michelle would move away and she would marry a man named Rusty Hart. The couple would have two daughters until their divorce in 1996.

The single mom worked as a dental assistant to support her daughters. Times were tight until 1999 when she met and married Steve Davis.

"Steve Davis was a businessman," Brion said. "He was divorced himself with a daughter of his own. He met Michelle and quickly fell for her charms as she could come across as a very warm and caring person. He asked her to marry him after about a year of dating."

Michelle would become pregnant during the union and give birth to her third daughter, Alyssa.

Unfortunately, her second marriage met the same fate as her first and within a few years, the couple had filed for divorce, citing irreconcilable differences.

Britt did well for himself after high school, becoming an airline mechanic for Delta Airlines. He made good money with Delta until they laid him off. He then went into business with his father in home construction until ultimately returning back to Delta after they had a rehire.

His marriage started to fail, however. His first wife cited that Britt had "mental problems" and filed for divorce, stating that the marriage was "irretrievably broken."

"Britt's first wife would take him to court at least six to eight times a year after their divorce," Brion said. "He was depressed and the court visits weren't helping."

His divorce would coincide with Michelle's impending divorce with Steve Davis. Her divorce with Davis was a particularly nasty one and Britt could sympathize. They would reconnect over a dating website.

In the midst of her own divorce, Garner was happy to find love again with Britt Hall as they rekindled old flames. Shortly after reconnecting, Britt invited Michelle over for Sunday lunch with his family, and all seemed well for the couple.

"Michelle did mention to Britt's family that she was going through some difficult times with her divorce," Brion said. "She was cheerful throughout but hinted that the custody battles she was going through were quite serious."

Little did Britt Hall's family know that their excitement would soon be turned to devastation; a tragedy that would make national headlines and be detailed in various murder documentaries.

THE BRADY BUNCH

Ronald Hall, Britt's father was all to happy to have Michelle back in his son's life. At least at first.

"We visited and talked," Ronald said. "And she came in and was just as happy as she ever was," he said.

It wasn't long before Britt Hall's romance with Garner turned more serious, and the two tied the knot in September of 2006. The new marriage was an adjustment, to say the least. Britt had three children from his previous marriage and Michelle Hall had three of her own children as well. The blended family of eight was now living in Britt Hall's town home.

"You can imagine how tight the living quarters were," Brion said. "But Michelle's girls really took to their new stepfather. They became comfortable enough to call him 'Dad'."

Britt wanted a bigger home and decided to build a large home with the help of his father. The men paid for contractors to pour concrete and establish the foundation, but father and son built the majority of the house by hand.

"People didn't know where the couple were getting the money to build the house," Brion said. "But Britt did most of the work himself after the foundation was laid. So he was able to save a lot of money when it came to sweat equity. That's a testimony to how badly he wanted the marriage between he and Michelle to work out."

When all was said and done, Britt and Michelle Hall were the proud owners of a beautiful 4100 square foot home on ten acres, the perfect place to spend the rest of their lives together. The brand new house boasted vaulted ceilings, granite counter tops, and a finished basement. The construction would prove to be a house of cards, however, as things were brewing underneath the surface.

Michelle didn't have much luck with her two previous marriages, and although individual accounts may vary, her two former husbands are both to have reported being abused by Michelle during the course of their marriage.

Michelle never had a firm grasp on her emotions and didn't handle anger well. These character flaws would not bode well for her life with

Britt. Dealing with both partners' ex-spousal issues including custody and visitation, Michelle and Britt found themselves tinkering on the edge of divorce after a few months into their marriage.

"The way Britt and Michelle handled their issues were different," said family friend Sue Mathis. "Michelle was quicker to speak her mind and a lot of times, Britt just wanted her to try to gain a little bit more self-control."

Dealing with his own ex-wife and their similar divorce problems, Britt Hall was also facing his own internal battles with depression. Although he wasn't often the instigator in their frequent arguments, he was known to fervently engage in the verbal conflicts. While this certainly wasn't conducive to a happy and fruitful marriage, Britt Hall made it clear to friends he would not give up on his family and the life he had built.

The next couple of years came with continued stress, intensified by financial worries after the Halls realized they had gotten too far deep in debt as a result of building their dream home. Notices of foreclosure, liens on the house, and over-extensions were haunting the couple and causing both spouses to hit a breaking point.

On July 30, 2008, it was another typical tense day in the Hall household. Friends say Britt Hall, already aggravated due to a landscaper failing to complete a job on time, went to the store to pick-up hot dogs for a family get-together.

"Hey hon," Britt said as he called his wife. "How many hot dogs do you think I should get-"

"Count how many damn people are here," Michelle snapped. "That's how much you should get."

This would be the snide comeback that would break the straw in Britt's back. He grew tired at her constant bickering and baiting. When he came home that evening, a fight would ensue.

Michelle's youngest daughter, Alyssa, was in the living room watching television as her mother vacuumed to prepare for the company soon arriving. When Britt Hall told Alyssa to turn the TV down, another argument between the couple ensued and Hall immediately told her daughter to go upstairs to her bedroom and not come out until she was called.

There are only two individuals who know the details of what followed on that evening, and only one of them lived to tell. When all was said and done, Britt would be dead and Michelle would be charged with murder.

The 911 call came in at 8:02 p.m. by a frantic Michelle who told dispatchers that her husband had tried to kill her and commit suicide.

"He shot at me, and we were fighting to get it," Michelle told dispatchers regarding the weapon. She said she heard the gun go off twice. Seconds later, she told dispatchers her husband was turning blue.

When police arrived, Britt Hall was dead and had three noticeable gunshot wounds to his body: one on his left arm, one on his right thigh, and a close-range shot to his chest. Michelle Hall, bruised, scraped and covered in blood, told first responders the same story she had told dispatchers: her suicidal husband had tried to kill her before turning the gun on himself.

Prior to further investigation, deputies on the scene immediately called Britt Hall's parents and told them their son had committed suicide. The Halls refused to believe the news.

"Things just seemed to be going too good at this time in his life for him to have done that," said his mother, Charlene Hall. "I knew he didn't kill himself; I knew for a fact that didn't happen."

It didn't take long for police to begin seeing the crime scene a little differently than Michelle had described. Blood splatter and numerous bullet holes covered the downstairs bedroom, and a trail of blood led into the bathroom where Britt Hall's lifeless body now lay. If this was a suicide, there sure was a struggle beforehand.

Investigators gave Michelle the opportunity to explain the scene. She told how an argument between the couple turned violent when

Britt Hall threw her onto the bed. He immediately went into the study and she followed him.

Then she noticed the gun on the computer desk.

Knowing her husband was battling depression, she said she immediately became concerned with his safety, worried that he may use the gun to harm himself.

Michelle stated that she instinctively dove for the gun, and that's when Britt Hall reached for it as well and the two began struggling for possession.

After both Michelle and her husband lost control of he gun, she quickly picked up the weapon and began shooting rounds into the walls and floor in an effort to unload the gun.

In the hall, Britt Hall caught up with her and that's when she said he threatened to kill her. In yet another entanglement of an attempt for control of the gun, Michelle said the gun accidentally went off. This shot punctured Britt Hall's thigh, and that's when Hall claimed she went to call for help.

Britt Hall began crawling into the bathroom, unable to walk and calling out her name for help. When she approached him, gun in hand, she said he grabbed the pistol from her, put it to his chest, and pulled the trigger.

The problem with her story, however, was that most suicides don't entail multiple gunshot wounds. Additionally, the manner in which the fatal shot was delivered raised eyebrows for investigators.

"I've worked many suicides in my career, and I've never worked a suicide that I can remember where a man had shot himself in the chest," Lt John Lewis said.

Furthermore, the gunshot wound on Britt Hall's chest had no signs of charring or burning around the entry wound, signs which usually indicate a self-inflicted wound.

Britt Hall also had a shattered elbow and a bullet hole in his left arm. Three different shots, all which led investigators to believe they weren't being told the whole story.

Michelle did her best to persuade the investigative team to believe her story, but her story changed upon being brought to the station for questioning. While at first she claimed the two struggled for control over the gun, she then claimed Britt Hall was never actually in possession of the gun at all.

Coupled with the evidence at the crime scene and her story's inconsistencies, Michelle was charged the next morning with the murder of her husband.

Crucial to the prosecution's case was the testimony of Michelle's youngest daughter, Alyssa, who was in the home during the shooting. Police brought the 8-year-old in for questioning immediately following the incident and she clearly stated she heard her step-father pleading with her mother to "put the gun down," she said. Alyssa would ultimately testify in her mother's trial in 2009.

Facing charges of malice murder and aggravated assault, Michelle vehemently denied killing her husband. She insisted that he died of a self-inflicted gunshot wound after threatening suicide and fighting with her over the .38 caliber revolver.

The fight that evening was par for the course, she said. The two regularly got into verbal and physical altercations, and their marriage was falling apart due to financial stress. They would also constantly fight over ex-spouses, custody and visitation regarding the six children. Although there were no police reports relating to any domestic altercations in the home before, family and friends knew things weren't okay on the home front.

"Britt would spend several nights driving to work calling me and saying 'I don't know what to do.' He would have done everything in his power to save his marriage, even if it was not worth saving. He was terrified of failure," said Mathis.

One of the first fights that turned physical in front of the family was in November 2006, when Britt Hall's eldest daughter came into the room to find Michelle Hall unconscious. Her father quickly ushered her out of the room and told her not to worry about it. The next couple of years only brought more trouble due to the same old problems and Britt's alleged mental illness.

Britt was prescribed three different types of medication for depression at the time of his death, police confirmed.

But the physical evidence did not add up to suicide. Initially, the Georgia Bureau of Investigation estimated the fatal gunshot to have been fired from around 18-24 inches away. This is not consistent with suicide, detectives argued. While many victims of mental illness fall prey to suicide each year, the facts must add up. In this case, they did not.

If convicted, Michelle was facing life in prison.

In September of 2009, testimonies were heard by Alyssa Davis, as well as responding officers Capt. Tony Grant and Sgt. Freddy Cox, about what they saw and heard on the night of the shooting.

Cox testified that Hall's appearance was "consistent with someone who'd been in a physical altercation" and that Hall had bruises, scrapes and blood on her neck and forehead as well as blood on her hands and a knot on her elbow.

During his testimony, Grant stated he immediately noticed that Hall's face was red and she had what appeared to be gun-shot residue on her hand, even though she was stating her husband had committed suicide.

There were multiple bullet holes throughout the downstairs of the home when police arrived on the scene, Grant testified. Two bullets were recovered from Britt Hall's body and three more were found in the house.

Grant said a blood pattern analysis showed blood spatters of 90 degrees in the downstairs quarters outside of the bathroom, proof that Britt Hall crawled into the bathroom after being wounded.

Defense Attorney Mike Kam said that while in no uncertain terms would he call the key ear witness a liar, her age and her location during the shooting did not make for the most reliable testimony.

"She was eight; she didn't see anything, she clearly got some of the facts confused." Kam said in an interview. "She's not someone who is used to being asked questions in formal interview settings. Who knows what she remembered, or what happened?"

Additionally, Kam indicated that Michelle certainly didn't fit the description of a murderer. Outside of two divorces, Hall had no criminal record. She was law-abiding citizen, with nothing in her background which would give the assumption she was capable of murder, he said.

But the jury had heard enough. On September 25, 2009, Michelle Hall was found guilty on all counts in the death of her husband Britt.

Not long after her conviction, Hall's attorneys filed a motion for a new trial, citing trial court errors. Coweta County Superior Court Judge Jack Kirby denied the motion and the defense attorneys took the case to the Supreme Court.

On September 22, 2010, the Supreme Court of Georgia upheld the conviction, despite Hall's defense's argument that the trial court erred by admitting similar transaction evidence and prior consistent statements.

Hall's defense stated that testimony from both of her ex-husbands that she was verbally and physically abusive were inadmissible because they were not "sufficiently similar" to establish proof of the crimes for which she was charged, according to the opinion of the Supreme Court. It also stated that "in cases of domestic violence, prior incidents of abuse against family members or sexual partners are more generally permitted because there is a logical connection between violent acts against two different persons with whom the accused had a similar emotional or intimate attachment."

The opinion also added that the fifteen and thirteen-year lapses of time between her ex-husband's allegations of abuse to the alleged shooting of her husband did not require exclusion of evidence.

"Given that the similar transaction evidence reflects appellant's behavior towards prior spouses, we conclude that any prejudice from the age of these prior incidents was outweighed by the probative value of the evidence under the particular facts of this case and the purpose for which the similar transactions were offered."

Eighteen months later, however, Michelle retained a new attorney who filed a habeas corpus petition, stating Michelle was given ineffective legal counsel by Kam during her trial in 2009. Senior Judge Robert B. Struble presided over the hearing and determined that Hall was in-fact entitled to a new trial. Struble agreed that Kam, Hall's trial attorney, was "ineffective and fell below the minimum guarantee of representation under the constitution," a press release said.

While Michelle may have been looking forward to another chance at redemption, The Attorney General's Office quickly announced their plans to appeal the habeas corpus ruling to the Georgia Supreme Court.

In a press release on March 30, 2012, Coweta County District Attorney Peter John Skandalakis expressed his respectful disapproval of the court's ruling and that in stating Kam was ineffective for representation, "the court erroneously applied the wrong standard under the law."

Skandalakis said he was optimistic that the Supreme Court will conclude that Hall had a legally sufficient defense and that her conviction would be upheld after review of the appeal.

On January 22, 2013, the Supreme Court found Hall's convictions to be fair and just, denying insufficient representation during her 2009 trial. According to the court summary, the Supreme Court concluded that the habeas corpus petition did not conduct proper legal analysis to determine the effectiveness of Hall's defense.

The opinion references Strickland v. Washington, a 1984 Supreme Court case in which it determined that to be granted a new trial, a defendant must show that it was due to insufficient performance by defense that the defendant was found guilty.

Michelle's argument for her habeas corpus petition was that "if she were in the same room when her young daughter was questioned, she could have assisted her attorney by prompting him with specific information," the court says in its opinion. However, it was determined during the habeas hearing that any information she would have portrayed to her attorney was already known information to both parties. "As such, Hall has failed to show actual prejudice, and her claim of ineffective assistance of counsel should have been rejected," the opinion said.

Today, Michelle Hall remains in a Coweta County prison.

Since her conviction, Michelle's ex-husbands have been given full custody of her three respective daughters.

She won't be eligible for parole until 2039. She will be 70 years old.

www.ingramcontent.com/pod-product-compliance
Lightning Source LLC
LaVergne TN
LVHW091046150826
845673LV00002B/483